FEAR NOT TO SOW

LIST OF SUBSCRIBERS

Mr. and Mrs. T. J. Allan, Lanarkshire
Annie T. Altschul, Edinburgh
James Anderson, Cambridge
Robin Anderson, Cambridge
Esther M. Armstrong, Stirlingshire
A.E.A. Atherton, Northumberland
Margaret Gibson Auld, Peeblesshire
Roger C. Bailey, Gwent
David H. Bayes, Edinburgh
Colleen Breck, Orkney
British Red Cross Museum & Archives
Dame Anne Bryans, British Red Cross, London
Melissa and Philip Budden, Cornwall
Margaret B. Burnett (nee Hewitt), Argyll
M. Christie, Stirlingshire
D. A. Charlton, Northumberland
Peter & Norah Clark, Edinburgh
Community Central Hall, Glasgow
Jenny Corrigall, Cambridge
Mary Robertson Duncan, Glasgow
George Findlay, Dumfries
Morag C. Findlay, Edinburgh
Mary W. Findlow, Oxfordshire
The Forth Valley College of Nursing & Midwifery, Stirlingshire
Catherine M. Fraser, Edinburgh
Margaret Freeman, Northumberland
Jeanette Fyfe, Fife
James D. C. Geddes, West Lothian
John R. Gibbon, London
Helen L. Gichard, Powys
Margaret Gilmore, Edinburgh
Glasgow University Department of Adult & Continuing Education
Winifred Logan Gordon, Glasgow
Nancy Grant, Canada
Anne Gray, Paisley
Pamela Grosvenor, Hampshire
Alastair & Margaret Heron, Sheffield
E. W. Himsworth, East Kilbride
Lisbeth Hockey, Edinburgh
Mrs. Constance Holt, Isle of Man
Katherine Hunter, Oxfordshire
L. N. Jamieson, Shetland
Mrs. M. M. Johnstone, Edinburgh
Joy Heron Kor, Colorado, U.S.A.
Daphne M. Laing, Dundee

B. Leckie, Glasgow
Morag Liebert, Edinburgh
Elsie P. Lister, Edinburgh
Isabella S. Lister, Edinburgh
Margaret Janet Longphee, Glasgow
Lothian College of Nursing & Midwifery, South Division, Edinburgh
Ann L. Marrs, Norfolk
Mrs. Wilma MacDonald, Edinburgh
Dorothy J. McClements, Falkirk
Helen McDonald, Australia
Sandra McSwein, Hampshire
Elisabeth Nicolson (nee Booth), Shetland
Norfolk College of Nursing & Midwifery
Diana Christine Paul (now West), Birmingham
Phoebe C. L. Pinder-Houghton (nee Gould), Lancashire
Mrs. Ann Pugh, Edinburgh
Jean W. Rafferty, Glasgow
Norma Ramsay, Glasgow
Esther Reid, Edinburgh
Nancy Roper, Edinburgh
Phyllis Runciman, Edinburgh
Anne B. Russell, Sheffield
Janet Russell, Edinburgh
Muriel Scarth, The Netherlands
Heidi Schaerz, Switzerland
Fiona D. Shepherd, Dundee
E. Short, Northumberland
Helen Sinclair, Edinburgh
Penelope Skinner (nee Robertson), Surrey
Eileen M. Stephenson, Norfolk
Henry Stephenson (brother Harry), Hertfordshire
Peter G. M. Stephenson, Norfolk
Robert M. Stephenson, Norfolk
Allan Story, Newcastle upon Tyne
Lilias A. M. Strang, Glasgow
Elisabeth Stussi, WHO Regional Office for Europe
Billie Thomson, Edinburgh
Margaret W. Thomson, Edinburgh
Alison J. Tierney, Edinburgh
Corinna Tyagi, Glasgow
Wincenty Tylmanowski, Poland
Rose van den Berg, The Netherlands
West Suffolk Hospital, Bury St. Edmunds
Moira T. Wadsworth, Glasgow
Henry & Sula Walton, Edinburgh
Rosemary Weir, Edinburgh
Sarah K. Whitcher, Cambridgeshire
Maureen White, Hampshire
Stewart & Elizabeth White, Glasgow
Kathleen J. W. Wilson, Peebles

Sheila Allan

Fear Not to Sow

The Story of Elsie Stephenson,
First Director of University Nursing Studies in Europe

With a Foreword by
ANNIE ALTSCHUL

THE JAMIESON LIBRARY
NEWMILL, PENZANCE, CORNWALL

First Published 1990
© by Sheila Allan

Published for the Jamieson Library by the
Patten Press
The Old Post Office
Newmill, Penzance, Cornwall TR20 4XN

ISBN 1 872229 05 0

To my family, Malcolm, Fay and Heather, and to my
parents, Peter and Norah

Printed in Great Britain by
Billings & Sons Ltd.
Worcester

Contents

List of Illustrations

Foreword

When I first heard Elsie Stephenson speak in 1962, I came from that meeting persuaded of the urgent work which needed to be done, for the Health Service, the nursing profession, and the sick and healthy all over the world. Without the faintest idea of what exactly should be done, I suddenly felt enthused and impatient to get going. Immediately I felt not only responsible but also capable to act. Even so short an exposure to Elsie Stephenson had the effect on me which Sheila Allan so vividly highlights in the book and to which all who knew Elsie testified.

I worked with Elsie Stephenson for only three years. For more than 20 years I have been mourning her death. Many who knew Elsie still experience a sense of loss. Speaking and writing about Elsie helps to work through such persistent grief.

Sheila Allan was motivated to write by the need to come to terms with Elsie's death. The story is highly evocative. Those who knew Elsie will read the book with much pleasure and will vividly recall the part they themselves played in Elsie's life.

This biography will be of interest also to those who never knew the dynamism of Elsie Stephenson. There is at present much interest in the place of women in recent history. There is an upsurge in interest in the history of nursing. With a great sense of urgency young nurses collect evidence from elderly members of the profession in order to capture, before it is too late, some of the vision, dedication and commitment which motivated British nurses in the early part of this century. No account of the history of nursing can be complete, which does not allocate pride of place to Elsie Stephenson.

It is, regrettably, too late to have Elsie speak for herself. Sheila Allan's story brings Elsie to life through quotations from her writings and from the mouths of those who knew her and whose lives took on new meaning as a result.

Historians will be grateful to Sheila Allan. It is my hope that young nurses too will be glad the book was written. Perhaps some of them will, when reading it, experience a faint tingling sensation in response to Elsie Stephenson's vibrant, effervescent vitality.

Annie T. Altschul CBE, FRCN
RGN, RMN, RNT, BA, M.Sc.
Emeritus Professor of Nursing Studies
University of Edinburgh

There are those who give little of the much which they have - and they give it for recognition and their hidden desire makes the gift unwholesome.

And there are those who have little and give it all.

These are the believers in life and the bounty of life, and their coffer is never empty.

There are those who give with joy, and that joy is their reward. And there are those who give with pain, and that pain is their baptism.

And there are those who give and know not pain in giving, nor do they seek joy, nor give with mindfulness of virtue.

They give as in yonder valley the myrtle breathes its fragrance into space.

From the hands of such as these God speaks, and from behind their eyes smiles upon the earth.

"The Prophet" by Kahlil Gibran (1883 - 1931)

Introduction

In the late 1950s and early 1960s, Edinburgh's newspapers ran occasional articles on a new university Nursing Studies Unit. The Unit's Director, a Miss Elsie Stephenson, was quoted as saying that academic girls should consider nursing as a career, since nurse training was now moving into the higher education sector.

The idea appealed to academically able girls whose schools, at a time when educational opportunities were burgeoning, could suggest little beyond teaching or the civil service as possible careers. Girls of this first post war generation were vaguely aware that their future held possibilities beyond the imaginings of their parents; parents who had lived through World War II wanted their children to know a better world than they themselves had known; and so an academic approach to the noble profession of nursing seemed the answer to some of those who sought wider opportunities.

As one of the integrated degree course students, I was strongly influenced by Miss Stephenson. She was a little woman, stout, and with penetrating brown eyes. When she spoke, you felt that you were the only person in the world who mattered to her. Immediately, you became one of her "family", and your well-being became her main concern. She was seldom too busy to speak to a student.

Attending one of Elsie's lectures was an unforgettable experience, not so much for its content as for its manner of delivery. She seldom referred to notes, and she spoke slowly and in simple language, but with such conviction that she filled her listeners with enthusiasm for the role of nursing in society. She was somehow able to demystify health issues while ennobling simple modes of behaviour in such a way that these came within the grasp of everyone.

"What keeps you healthy?" she asked our class early in our training. We suggested immunisations, surgical advances, antibiotics. She looked at us gravely.

"What about food, a safe water supply, shelter, warmth?"

At the time we felt a touch of resentment that she had not acknowledged our suggestions as useful contributions to our health and well-being. After all, we argued, in a university department of nursing, one might expect to learn about the latest techniques in medicine and the most sophisticated advances in science. But Elsie's message was clear: there was nothing mysterious about good nursing practice; it demanded simply the combination of compassion for other human beings with the application of sound knowledge of health matters. Nurses would continue to deal with the mundane, everyday lives of ordinary people. Except that in Elsie's hands the mundane was exotic, and every individual's life a precious gift to be treasured.

In 1983, Edinburgh University was celebrating its 400th anniversary. Along with multitudes of other graduates, I returned to attend open days in some of the departments where I had spent my student days. The Nursing Studies Department still housed in the Adam Ferguson Building had put on a show for its visitors. Time and effort had been spent preparing exhibitions of work done in the research field; books written by members of the Department were on display; students, somehow persuaded to appear during vacation time, delivered an illuminating slide show on their recent visit to health centres in India; Professor Annie Altschul, about to retire, delivered a lecture on "Nostalgia for the Good Old Days";

and, most significant for me, a sample from the Elsie Stephenson Collection from the Medical Archive Centre was on display.

I was absorbed. Here I found a focus for thoughts about the early days of the Nursing Studies Unit and Elsie Stephenson's role as the first Director of the Department. Bill Gardner, her widower, had kept in touch with me after her death while he was collecting information for his planned biography on Elsie. Sadly, he died before achieving that goal.

Helping Professor Altschul paste up pages of photographs of former staff and students, I recalled the uniquely personal relationship between staff and students in this Department, a tradition which Elsie had firmly established. I mentioned to the Professor how much the extracts of the Elsie Stephenson Collection had affected me, and how I would love to be involved in piecing together a biography of Elsie. "Why don't you do it then?" she asked. Why indeed?

Thanks to Phyllis Runciman's cataloguing of the material, I found the Elsie Stephenson Collection in comprehensible order, although where to start on twenty-two boxes of papers was a problem. Bill Gardner had left names and addresses of contacts, plus letters and the transcripts of interviews gathered for the biography. This was fortunate since I was unable to trace some of her friends and colleagues.

As the picture of Elsie unfolded, I discovered the strength of conviction and purpose on which she had built the foundations. For my own part, I discovered something of the historical role we students had played in the early days of this department, with its present boast of fine publications, articulate students and remarkable academic nurses.

A biography is the story of a life, usually of someone outstanding. In a historical sense, Elsie was that, in that she headed the first university department for nurses in western Europe. But I am sure she would want to be remembered too as someone ordinary, someone who simply loved life and loved people. The life and warmth of Elsie Stephenson have been difficult to capture on paper, and the best I can hope is that this biography will remind her many friends of her sheer vibrancy, and show how an ordinary and determined woman makes history.

Chapter 1

A Rebel is Born

Fear Not to Sow

Elsie was born on 22nd January, 1916, at Crawleas Farm in County Durham, the youngest child and only daughter of Henry and Ethel Stephenson. By the end of the First World War, family life appeared to be returning to normal for the Stephensons. Elsie's three brothers, Harry, George and Willie were able to help on the farm, to which the labourers were gradually coming home from the battlefields.

Tragedy struck when Elsie was only two, however, and her father died in the influenza pandemic which took an estimated 27 million lives throughout the world. The 15 to 35 year age group, already decimated by war, accounted for 45% of the influenza casualties. "The disease simply had its way," it was said by one doctor. "It came like a thief in the night and stole treasure."[1]

Mrs. Stephenson, a strong, able woman, might have continued to run the farm alone. For a woman, however, such a move would have seemed quite unconventional at that time. It was the boys' horse riding enthusiasm that eventually decided the family's future. After living for a time in Aycliffe, they finally moved to Newmarket where all three Stephenson boys were able to develop their passion for horses. Willie eventually became a successful jockey and stable owner.

Although there were no other nurses in the Stephenson family, Elsie, as a child, was always dressing up as a nurse, and tending her dolls. She later claimed that she decided at the age of three to be a nurse. The climate in which she was taking her childish decision was quite remarkable. With an unconscious sense of timing she was mapping out her future in the same year in which her father died in a public health disaster, women were newly endowed with the right to vote, the professional status of nurses was being enhanced, (with the passing of the Nurses' Registration Act), and women's role in promoting public health work was being discussed at the Red Cross Convention in Cannes.

Her school days came and went. She attended St. Mary's Junior School, Newmarket, and then Newmarket Grammar School from 1926 until 1933. When she left school, her public examination record card stated: "Camb. S.C. Fail. July 1933", and her occupation after leaving: "Home Duties".[2] Few other records of those days survive. School photographs, however, depict a surprisingly bored-looking girl. The contrast with later photographs, where her expression glows with purpose and conviction, is quite startling.

Three years before leaving school, she joined the Newmarket branch of the Red Cross as a Voluntary Aid member.[3] Judging from her later performance as a Red Cross worker during and after the war, she took to heart the principles and aims she was taught at Red Cross classes. Perhaps her father's death had brought home to her the personal devastation attributable to ill health. Perhaps also her frequent contacts with church and Sunday school had awakened in her a spirit of service. Whatever the roots, her determination to become a nurse was unshakable.

Her path was by no means easy. The family was keen for her to stay at home and help her mother, who by now was fifty-nine years old, and not in the best of health. Elsie had a strong sense of family loyalty. It was Elsie, for instance, who stayed up for several nights in succession to nurse a niece injured in an accident. There can be no doubt that pressure from the family to stay at home caused her much heartache. Diary entries and letters from her training days and throughout her years abroad tell of some of the strains brought about by the conflict between work and home.

Despite the pressure from family and her own developed sense of duty, she began training at the West Suffolk General Hospital, Bury St. Edmunds, in May, 1935, at the age of 19, an average age for starting nurse training at that time.[4] The choice of the local voluntary hospital suggests that she was still keen to keep in touch with the family, and the West Suffolk, as hospitals went, was a friendly enough institution in which to train. Margaret Freeman, Elsie's friend from those days, feels there was something special about the atmosphere at the West Suffolk General Hospital:

"When I think of it, we had a very good training, and a lot of us had very forward ideas about what we wanted nursing to be. I really think the foundation was laid there."[5]

It was not uncommon for student nurses to develop a fierce loyalty towards their own training school. Simply to embark on the training presupposed a certain sense of vocation. Nurses in training could expect to work 119 hours a fortnight, to attend lectures during off-duty hours, to take part in the fundraising activities on which voluntary hospitals depended for their very existence, and as reward, to be paid £20 for the first year of training, £25 for the second, and £30 for the third.[6] Under these circumstances, student nurses had very little independence. They had little money to spend during whatever time they could call their own, and many of them were still dependent on their families for treats and holidays. Elsie appears to have adapted to the strictures of student nurse life reasonably well, throwing herself wholeheartedly into any extramural activity being organised for the nurses.

"Elsie was a great help to me in arranging programmes for our parties in the Nurses' Home..." Miss Agnes Scott, her tutor recalls. "In the summer we would have picnics after duty. We would hire a bus, pack our evening meal, specially

3

arranged for our picnic, and drive out a few miles, usually to Hardwick Heath, where having eaten our meal, we would have games, races, singsongs, until it began to get dark."[7]

For the patients, she enjoyed administering the little extra attentions, such as boiling face cloths or washing hair brushes. Sister of Holden Ward was none too impressed all the same, and remarked, "Nurse still thinks she is playing a game."[8]

Stories of the games she played show her as an incorrigible practical joker. Her brother Harry is fortunately still able to laugh at the time he came home to find Jimmy, the hospital skeleton, snugly tucked up in his bed. Elsie's energy and sense of fun were her means of survival in the institution where she spent her days and nights. In later years, she would see the shortcomings of that system of nurse training and use her power and influence to try to make changes for the better. At the time, she simply adapted to the situation and made the most of it.

Moves were already afoot, however, to try to remedy some of the ills of the nurse training system. The registration of nurses had highlighted an acute shortage throughout the 1920s and 1930s. The Lancet Commission, composed of representatives of the nursing and medical professions, hospital managers, educational authorities, and women's organisations, was set up in 1930, "to inquire into the reasons for the shortage of candidates, trained and untrained, for nursing the sick in general and special hospitals throughout the country, and to offer suggestions for making the service more attractive to women suitable for this necessary work."[9]

Among its findings there is criticsm of the host of petty restrictions and regulations dominating the lives of student nurses both in and out of hospital, such as the compulsory attendance at meals in 58% of hospitals, the fact that in 84% of hospitals nurses were not allowed out after 10 p.m. without a late pass, and that 33% of hospitals did not have separate bedrooms for probationers.[10]

In 1937, the Government set up the Athlone Committee "to inquire into the arrangements at present in operation with regard to the recruitment, training and registration and terms and conditions of service of persons engaged in nursing the sick and to report whether any changes in these arrangements or any other measures are expendient for the purpose of maintaining an adequate service both for institutional and domiciliary service."[11]

Not surprisingly, there were also some moves towards the setting up of trade unions for nurses during the 1920s and 30s. Nurses were, however, difficult to mobilise in the direction of collective bargaining, partly because their working conditions narrowed their view of life, and left them tired and short of cash, and partly because they were a dedicated band of people who would stop short of action that might harm their patients.

Even their own College of Nursing (which had been set up in 1916 and received a Royal Charter in 1937) failed to encourage nurses in training to assert their right to decent pay and conditions. The College reported to the Athlone Committee in the following terms: "The payment of high salaries to student nurses is not recommended, as it is believed that this does not tend to attract the most suitable type of candidate. The College prefers to consider the nurse in training as a student preparing for a career, receiving professional training practically free of cost and being provided with her maintenance when in hospital together with a small salary. The value of board, lodging, tuition and medical attention given to student nurses is not always realised by parents and guardians, who are apt to have regard only to the monetary return obtainable for services."[12]

Inherent in this statement is the assumption that student nurses are the property of their families, on loan to their training hospital for the duration of nurse training. The idea that student nurses might be independent young women, intent on making their contribution to the affairs of the world had apparently not yet influenced the College's policies. Yet any girl who was prepared to flout the wishes of her family, in the way that Elsie had done, in order to train as a nurse, was unlikely to take kindly to being patronised in this way.

The difficulty for any nurse wishing to challenge the status quo has always been that her choice of nursing as a career reduces the strength of her case for independence. Elsie, too, fell into this trap. As a caring professional, she would have suffered pangs of conscience if she had cut herself off from the family altogether. Besides which, she was a genuinely loving person. And so she had to live with her conviction that she was being tied by a kind of moral blackmail, while at the same time cherishing the ties that bound her. The maturity required to live peacefully with such conflict demanded much of these young student nurses, especially as they were being treated as overgrown schoolgirls in their daily lives. Small wonder that, now and then, the only recourse was to indulge in schoolgirl pranks.

The other claim in the Royal College of Nursing statement that Elsie would later challenge was that student nurses were in fact receiving "professional training" in the 1930s. Elsie was often to describe student nurses in the apprenticeship system of training as "so-called students." In fact, nurses in training were essential pairs of hands in the wards and departments of the hospitals, and often had to choose between remaining on duty to help with a critical situation, and going to attend lectures essential for their education.

Any move to change the system was further bedevilled by the fact that, once through the system, many nurses tended to adopt the attitude, "If it was good enough for us, it's good enough for the next lot." The wastage rate of 26-28% in 1930[13] among student nurses reflects the fact that many were not willing or able to continue against the odds. Those who did remain in training were likely to be those who would not be too upset if nothing changed in the nursing world, those who were so dedicated to the job that they would endure anything in order to be able to nurse, or those with no alternative.

Elsie, with her buoyant, gregarious nature, and her determination to nurse, was a survivor. Her sister tutor remembers one occasion when she did try to buck the system. Although student nurses accepted that they must attend lectures even during their off-duty, Elsie asked Miss Scott if she could be excused the lecture the following day.

"I hated having to refuse the request. I knew only too well how she felt, but, as I explained to her, it would be unfair to her colleagues and would create a precedent. My refusal was accepted with a grin and the remark, 'Oh well, it was worth a try'."

The occasion was Elsie's birthday. She had invited most of her classmates to her party, and they had all been brought to the lecture from the party by car. Miss Scott recalls that Elsie took a collection at the party in aid of hospital funds.[14]

No sooner had she finished general training in July, 1938, than she started midwifery training, in August, at Queen Charlotte's Hospital in London. Her mother's wishes appear to have influenced the choice of a famous London hospital, even though Elsie and her friend Joyce Double had previously agreed together that they would train at St. Mary's in Newcastle.[15]

The break from home and familiar surroundings presented Elsie with a new challenge, one which she met with ease, according to Jenny Causer, who met her on their first day at

Queen Charlotte's "Elsie came and sat at my table. As she was walking towards me, I thought, 'What a lovely girl.'...I'm sure it was due to her that I stuck in and got through my exams. We used to ask each other questions after studying, and there was no monkey business for that half hour. I used to tell her she'd make a good Sister Tutor."[16]

By this time, Elsie's sense of purpose was becoming apparent to those around her. Jenny Causer later recalled how Elsie was: "eager to get on, and I could see then how farseeing she was. She planned to take infectious diseases, languages and public health work, and wanted to get round into other countries to see...the nursing world."[17]

Part of the training for midwives was on the district, and here Elsie excelled. Another colleague, Margaret Vaughan Jones, recalls how Elsie's interest in people's welfare shone through during her midwifery training days.

"Elsie happened to be at Queen Charlotte's over Christmas and in one of the wards was a mother of six children with a baby a few days old. (She came from a poor home.) Elsie became really interested in this little family. She visited their home and saw that the children had a wonderful Christmas, toys, eats and warm clothing. The mother on returning home was surprised to find such a difference in the children and home. Elsie continued to visit this family long after she left Queen Charlotte's Hospital."[18]

Nursing people in their own homes affected Elsie profoundly, and in later years, she often expressed the opinion that caring for people in the community was altogether more satisfying than the unnatural environment of hospitals. By the time she had finished her midwifery training, war between Germany and Britain was inevitable. Elsie returned to the West Suffolk General as a Staff Midwife and Relief Sister, and met again Joyce Double, who had completed her midwifery training at St. Mary's in

Newcastle. At the outbreak of war, the two agreed that they could not make any great contribution to the war effort while working at the West Suffolk. They decided to take public health training but discovered that they were too young. In the meantime, they enrolled for Fever Training at the Ipswich Isolation Hospital.[19]

While waiting to begin the Fever course, Elsie did some private midwifery work around Newmarket in December, 1939, and January, 1940. One of the cases she attended was the writer Barbara Cartland, who had left London in this first cold winter of the war to spend her confinement in the relative peace of Six Mile Bottom, just outside Newmarket.

Her spell at the Ipswich was among the least happy of Elsie's training days. Diary entries frequently mention worries about her mother, who was unsettled and unenthusiastic about Elsie's plans to go north to study public health. Bombs were dropping, and Elsie was often cold and homesick.

29th January, 1941. *Off 5 p.m. - tired out - caught 6.10 p.m. train home - arrived home 9.30 p.m. - air raid all the way.*

15th February, 1941: *Very fed up at the thought of night duty.*

20th February, 1941: *Letter from home to say Newmarket had been bombed badly on Tuesday. Went to ring up. Couldn't get through.*

For all that, there were some happy times, when she and Joyce Double would cycle to Felixstowe, and spend the day at the Hospital's beach hut, sunbathing, studying and picnicking.

Despite homesickness, guilt feelings about her mother, and the war, she began training as a health visitor in Newcastle in September, 1941. Although the Red Cross Convention of 1919 had heard about the great work that lay ahead for women in public health nursing, health visiting in the early 1940s still had the image of a service only for mothers and young children. The role of the health visitor was unclear to the public, and further clouded by the effects of the Midwives' Act of 1936, which required local authorities to provide a domiciliary midwifery service. Health visitors, too, were expected to have a midwifery qualification, and the distinct roles of the two workers had not been satisfactorily defined.[20] However keen Elsie was to undertake this training, therefore, she was entering a field which was in a state of flux, and whose role in furthering the nation's health was still somewhat unclear.

She did not lack creative ideas on the possible role of the health visitor, and now and again provoked a startled response from tutors on the course. Asked to summarise the principles which should underlie the ideal maternity service, Elsie wished to include the teaching of some elementary physiology and mothercraft to children of 13 to 14 years." The examiner felt that 15 to 16 years would be a more appropriate age for such instruction - an approach which has quickly become outmoded as society has become more permissive.

Elsie also had firm ideas on the least satisfactory area of health education.

"The care of the adolescent is the least satisfactorily carried out...It is the potential mother to be considered...Today there are numbers of girls with no knowledge of the care of infants, or of the skill required...If these girls had some regular medical care, and good sound advice on personal hygiene, health and well being, surely the future mothers would be more efficient and healthy individuals."

She had apparently escaped the habits of thought described by Brian Abel-Smith as so typical of nurses in the early part of the twentieth century:

"Students continued to see patients as individuals and as 'cases'; they had little or no contact with the family in its natural setting. What was basic to understanding the emotional problems of the patient had no place in the formal training for the Register. The policy of treating in the home as much sickness as possible was not reflected in the basic training of nurses."[21]

She was prepared to apply thought to the practice of nursing, and to suggest new directions in which health visiting might advance. Her preference for community work may have saved her from the most narrowing effects of hospital nursing, and the struggle with family and conscience through which she had passed may have helped her hold on to her early convictions. Already she was on the road to advocating that nurses must be thinkers as well as doers.

Chapter 2

A Listener, A Doer

Fear Not to Sow

Elsie practised as a health visitor and school nurse from April, 1942, until January, 1944. As soon as she arrived in West Suffolk, she made an impression on the Medical Officer of Health:

"Right from the start I recognised her outstanding ability as a Health Visitor. She had intelligence and initiative...Even then, her forte was teaching. She set up classes in the Senior Girls' Schools where she taught mothercraft and hygiene."[1]

As already mentioned, health visiting was still in a state of transition when Elsie was training in Newcastle. The basis of her enthusiasm for public health work may well have lain in her connections with the Red Cross, whose 1919 Cannes Conference Report had emphasised the important contribution of nurses in World War I and the new field of public health work opening up to them:

"The great service which the trained nurse has been in a position to render during this last war has brought nursing into a prominence which years of peace had not given it."[2]

From the documentation left from Elsie's spell as a health visitor around Newmarket and Exning, it is clear that she had found her niche in this growing field of nursing. It provided scope for her flair for teaching, for her interest in people and for her boundless energy. Not content with working the hours set for her, she volunteered to take over the midwifery work in Newmarket for a few weeks to allow the midwives their annual holiday. The County Medical Officer gave her a glowing testimonial:

"I cannot speak too highly of her work here...Her kindliness, commonsense, and tact gained for her the confidence of both patients and parents...

The School Medical Service was enhanced by Miss Stephenson's work and she was successful in securing the added interest and co-operation of the teachers...

In Health Education Miss Stephenson was particularly interested and successful, both in the course of her work and with outside organisations such as Youth Clubs, Girl Guides and Girls' Training Corps."[3]

It was during Elsie's time with West Suffolk County Council that an experiment was set up to teach mothercraft in a senior school. Elsie was selected for the job, ran the classes after office hours, and aroused such enthusiasm in teachers and pupils alike that the head teacher recommended mothercraft as part of the regular curriculum in all senior schools.

The Infant Welfare Clinic sessions had to be more than doubled, under Elsie's influence. Newmarket's Medical Officer of Health waxed lyrical in her praise:

"I can, without qualification, state that I have never known a Health Visitor who appreciably approached the enthusiasm, ingenuity and wholehearted service of Miss Stephenson, nor one who obtained results commensurate with the success which marked her ardour...My capacities are inadequate to describe the high regard in which she is held by the mothers of Newmarket, or the unique enthusiasm they displayed towards her at the conclusion of the most successful parties she organised for them and their children...

The children of the town revere and admire her - thanks to her efforts the 1300 schoolchildren are 100% diphtheria immunised, and of the 550 pre-school age children, any unimmunised can be counted on the fingers. On many occasions the general practitioners of the town have acknowledged that the recovery of their patients has been expedited by the help of this woman, who is a friend of all Newmarket families."[4]

Again it is interesting to view these testimonials to Elsie's success in the public health field in the light of Dr. Welch's predictions at the 1918 Cannes Red Cross Conference:

"In a sense no more important subject than nursing has been brought before the Red Cross Conference...Few realise as yet the career in Public Health nursing which is opening to women. It makes a strong appeal to many not attracted by private or hospital nursing. Women must guide this movement...There is...no agency through which more good can be done."[5]

Here was Elsie, during World War II, making that vision a reality. During the years of the war, when Elsie and her counterparts were working in the public health sector, Britain's most healthy generation yet was born. In spite of the bombing, 4.6 million children were born in Britain between 1939 and 1945. In 1939 the maternal mortality rate was 2.55 per thousand births, and the infant mortality rate 51 per thousand. By 1945 the figures were reduced to 1.53 per thousand maternal mortalities, and 45 per thousand infant mortalities.[6]

The health visitor's role in influencing the health of the nation continued to fascinate her throughout her life.

"Most Health Visitors chose this field," she told a Conference "as they realised that [total patient care] could only be accomplished by the appreciation of family needs in health and sickness." [7]

Even in 1956, when she spoke those words, she was ahead of the field in her appreciation of the health visitor's potential role. Not until 1965 were health visitors required to be trained nurses. Yet by the end of her public health training, Elsie saw her role clearly among ordinary people, living ordinary lives, which she hoped to be able to make safer, healthier and therefore happier.

Throughout her career, Elsie retained the enthusiasm she had first shown in her student days for educating young people to take on the role of parenthood. In 1962, addressing a conference, she said:

"The mother and infant in a maternity hospital, together with the husband should be in the closest contact. These are the families of the future, the real health educators of the future...Two people taking on the most important job in life, often with little or no preparation, surrounded by folklore and ignorance in some cases."[8]

Twenty years of experience of life had taught her how right she had been in her convictions as a student and newly-fledged health visitor, and in health visiting she found scope for the broad concept of nursing as she defined it in the 1960s:

"A listener, a doer, someone who tries to understand the physical, mental and spiritual needs of man from infancy to old age."[9]

Elsie's old tutor from the West Suffolk General Hospital fell into conversation with another passenger on the train to Scotland during the war years.

"She told me about her husband who had been invalided home from the war, about his intense depression, and his efforts to get back to a normal way of life. She went on to tell me of the Health Visitor who came to see him very frequently. She said she was a marvellous person. She had been such a help to her husband, giving him fresh encouragement and incentive to persevere. She said she couldn't speak too highly of her, and she knew that all her friends in the district felt the same way about her. When she finished the story, I asked her the name of her Health Visitor. 'A Miss Stephenson,' she said."[10]

There is no knowing how long Elsie would have remained as a health visitor in West Suffolk if she had not decided to join the war effort. By December, 1943, she was designated by the Red Cross as the only State Registered Nurse (S.R.N.) in a team destined for the Middle East.[11] In January, 1944, she left West Suffolk County Council, in preparation for work with the Civilian Relief group of the British Red Cross Society.

Chapter 3

War Work in Egypt

Fear Not to Sow

Before leaving Britain, Elsie received pages of instructions from the British Red Cross Society. The equipment for civilian relief workers included a steel helmet, a respirator and water bottle. Camp equipment was provided as follows:

- ☐ Valise and two straps
- ☐ Sleeping bag,
- ☐ 2 Sleeping bag linings
- ☐ Green ground sheet
- ☐ Camp bed
- ☐ Canvas bucket
- ☐ Mattress and pillow
- ☐ Mosquito net
- ☐ 2 blankets
- ☐ Mess tin
- ☐ Enamel plate and mug
- ☐ Knife, fork and spoon
- ☐ Thermos
- ☐ Torch
- ☐ Keating's powder
- ☐ First aid pack

Travel advice was practical and down to earth:

"Make your hand luggage as light as possible, since you will have a lot of standing around and walking to do from the time

you arrive at the station until you get on board. You will find that with your gas mask, tin hat and water bottle, you will get very tired."

While on board ship, relief workers were required to carry their lifebelts about with them.

"This reminds you of the possibility of being torpedoed, and having to take to the boats. If you are wise you will make some PERSONAL preparations for such an emergency yourself," the notes warned.

Suggestions included an old scarf or towel, which could be tied round the head turban-wise, and hung down the back of the neck, wetted with sea water, to protect against sun stroke.

Health hints covered methods of avoiding heat stroke, stomach and bowel problems, malaria, prickly heat, and foot troubles.

"You are undertaking most strenuous and exacting work, and will require all your health and strength. You should aim at keeping thoroughly well, and on top of your form. The best way to do this is by taking the precautions recommended to you."[1]

Small wonder, given all these warnings, that Elsie's diary betrays a certain apprehension before departure from Britain.

19th February, 1944. *Raid. Packed bits and pieces. I do hope I'm doing right.*

20th February, 1944. *Left King's Cross 12.45 a.m. for unknown destination - travelled to Liverpool, arrived 9.10 a.m. Eventually arrived on Strathkelvin 1.30 p.m.*

Twenty-four women, one of whom was Elsie, were included in the British Red Cross party which arrived in the Middle East in March, 1944, although the War Office had put up a stout protest against the use of women in civilian relief. Only with the help of the Civil Affairs Branch was this ban lifted, and Elsie therefore enabled to take her place.[2]

Refugees in the Middle East consisted of thousands of civilian victims of the war who, since 1942, had been streaming into refugee camps around Egypt. There were Poles from U.S.S.R., evacuees from Greece, Malta, Cyprus and various Balkan countries, the majority women and children, all arriving in conditions of immense distress.[3]

The party with which Elsie arrived in 1944 was part of the British Red Cross response to a request for cooperation from the Middle East Relief and Refuge Administration who were taking care of the refugees, assisted initially by the American Red Cross, the Greek Red Cross, and the Egyptian Red Crescent. Trained nurses with the British Red Cross were destined for such positions of responsibility as taking charge of a hospital.[4]

Elsie recorded in her diary her first impressions:

8th March, 1944. *First day in camp - not at all bad - right in middle of desert - Pyramids in sight and Citadel Old Cairo.*

This was the camp at Maadi where Middle East Relief and Refuge Administration trained Joint War Organisation personnel for work with U.N.R.R.A. (United Nations Relief and Rehabilitation Administration.) The two week training course consisted of lectures on purifying water, combatting typhus, dealing with medical stores, cooking on mobile field stoves, disinfesting people and villages of vermin. Added to these very practical instructions was information on the daily lives and politics of the refugees with whom they would be dealing.[5]

Practical experience followed the two weeks training at Maadi. For Elsie, this took the form of a three week spell as Night Superintendent in the refugee camp hospital at El Shatt.

26th March, 1944. *Sand everywhere - taken round hospital - 60 General and 60 isolation beds - feeling awful - in bed most of day - sand storm in progress.*

An eye problem had caused her illness, but she was able to go on night duty three days later, to supervise the birth of her "first Yugoslav baby", and to record how it was "strange in the desert doing night duty". At the end of her three weeks at El Shatt, Elsie set off in an open truck, through glorious orange blossom, for Khatatba refugee camp in the heart of the desert, where she would spend the next six months.

12th April, 1944. *First morning at Khatatba - called with tea, shoes cleaned - a good beginning - viewed hospital - not at all bad - a few alterations.*

The camp consisted of an old recreation hall and two chapels. Within two weeks of arrival, the Royal Engineers had rigged up a hospital of tents, with hot and cold water and electricity in wards. Equipment was unpacked, sorted, allotted to the various departments. On 25th April, Elsie and a R.A.M.C. sergeant made up 155 beds ready for admission. The remaining nursing staff arrived that evening. The hospital was ready for action.[6]

The recreation room had become the children's ward and male ward, of 35 beds. One chapel housed 15 female and maternity beds, while the other chapel was the labour ward. Eight tents containing a total of 90 beds made up the isolation block.

With a staff of two trained nurses, three V.A.D.s, one medical orderly, and five Syrian nurses (who spoke only Arabic and departed after undefined trouble on 27th April), life was indeed hectic. On 26th April, when the hospital opened, 68 patients were admitted, a number of them children who arrived with measles. Elsie ran the hospital block, did all the administrative work, and was on call at nights.

10th May, 1944. *Up all night. 15,000 more refugees - 24 admitted to hospital - all very ill - very tired.*

Nonetheless, she started an ante-natal clinic, booking 12 expectant mothers on the first day. She enlisted whatever help she could find. One of the most useful helpers was a Yugoslav trained midwife who was able to run the midwifery block with minimal supervision. Elsie also found 30 girls from the camp with sufficient reading and writing skills for her to train them in hygiene and give them practical demonstrations on the wards. Four girls, she discovered, had received one week's transit training in Italy, and she gave them extra practical training so that they could become charge nurses.

Epidemics of measles and whooping cough were contained by the prompt provision of isolation blocks. Soon the hospital accommodation was increased to 265 beds, and A.T.S. nurses' aides arrived to augment the staff.

Each tent in the camp housed 20 people, and 50 - 100 tents were arranged in a section with its own dining room, cook house, lavatories, and one main bath house for the whole camp. All sections were centred round the administration block and about a mile from the hospital unit and British Staff section.[7]

The mixture of staff and cultures put a great strain on relationships. There was a skeleton army staff of British, South Africans and Americans, Basuto guards from South Africa, and a multitude of voluntary organisations such as the British Red Cross, the American Red Cross, Jewish Relief, Save the Children Fund, Girl Guides, Boy Scouts, Friends' Ambulance Unit, International Society for Peace, Catholic Women's Relief Abroad, Kenya Red Cross, Egyptian nuns, cooks and workmen. Over the months U.N.R.R.A. personnel of various nationalities arrived, as well as Palestinian nurses' aides. The wonder is that they all managed to pull together. Elsie summed up how the challenge was met:

"Among all was the one aim, that was to help those in need, and this was a real bond of cooperation, and certainly smoothed out many difficulties."[8]

Elsie described the refugees as typical peasants who worked hard for their living and knew little of the riches of life. They were of fine physique and fond of music. Three-quarters of them were illiterate.

"This group of magnificent, brave, yet stricken people consisted of old men and women, boys and girls, babes in arms, young and expectant mothers...Young able boys and girls of 14 and upward...had stayed to help guard and fight for their homeland."[9]

The refugees, on arrival, were registered, issued with equipment and shown to their tents, where as far as possible natural groups were kept together.

"That first night of the arrival of these people will live forever in my memory, for the desert was alive with sad melodies...one could feel the yearning and the pride of these people for their homeland."[10]

The organisation of the camp was aimed at helping the refugees to run their own lives (a concept which might have been difficult for an authoritarian nursing figure to grasp, and yet came naturally to Elsie.) The Central Yugoslav Committee and the Central British Committee met daily, and soon self-government was achieved. Harmony was eased by the unifying adherence to Tito as leader. As community feeling grew, so did the facilities offered. A church was set up, and a school using one or two tents in each section. Welfare centres appeared - a tent in each section where infants were bathed, feeds made up, and advice given. A laundry, a barber shop, a valet service, sewing classes, shoe repairs and a carpenter arrived, as well as hygiene squads, a fire brigade, a labour bureau, sports club, newspaper, children's playground, camp guard, open air theatre and cemetery.[11]

Death was a fairly common occurrence, and each death was mourned with the traditional death wail. In spite of the lack of materials, the refugees managed somehow to make paper flowers for the dead.

"These would be really attractive. The dead must be fully clothed, even at a period when clothes and shoes were impossible to get; the dead must be clothed even if the living went without."[12]

While the administrators of the camp did their utmost to maintain the social structure familiar to the Yugoslavs in their care, there were occasions when the social divide was apparent. The Yugoslavs, for instance, were puzzled when relief workers assumed that the men would do the heavy work. Their tradition was the opposite. Elsie commented that it was quite common to see a mother carrying a son of seven or eight while his two year old sister walked behind. The whole camp celebrated the birth of a boy, but maintained a staunch silence over the birth of a girl.

An intricate social pattern began to emerge. Elsie noticed that certain groups would refuse to mix and certain areas of the camp would be reserved for the elite, even though all had escaped with the same minimum of personal belongings. She was interested in finding ways of reducing the differences between these conflicting groups, and, in her report to Dame Emily Blair and Miss Fernandez of the British Red Cross, she described a party organised for the arrival of her successor as hospital matron, during which all the refugees worked together. A later paper, written by Elsie at Toronto University, also described theatrical plays performed in the camp, depicting the life of the refugees' homeland, at peace and at war.

Weddings, she noted, were occasions for great intergroup activity. Items of value, such as Dalmatian embroidered cloths, handwoven Serbian rugs and wedding dresses were loaned or bartered. Paper flowers appeared as from nowhere, and greenery was produced by growing bean leaves in empty milk tins. She also remarked on how men and women used the opportunities on offer differently. The men played chess, listened to the radio, read magazines and took English lessons at the English cultural club, while the women and girls preferred to attend embroidery classes.

Once the hospital was well established, Elsie applied for a transfer to make better use of her public health training.

"I liked the work in the Hospital but felt my specialist training in Public Health could be utilised better by attempting to teach fuller health and doing infant welfare work in the camps and centres, and so my release was promised for July 1st."[13]

Now in her field of public health, Elsie inoculated 2,765 children with diphtheria anti-toxin, thus ensuring protection to all children in the camp between the ages of six months and twelve years. She made strenuous efforts to give the mothers at the infant welfare clinics sound preventive advice. Her success on this score can best be judged by the report of Captain Ryan in September, 1944.

"The onset of cooler weather...coincided with an improvement of the general health of the refugees. This improvement in the health and happiness of the people is no doubt due to a number of factors, but one of the most important of these was a higher standard of personal hygiene. The example of what the Infant Welfare Clinics were doing for the younger children in the way of increased cleanliness and prevention of disease was not lost to their elders.

Routine daily washing of over 600 children is carried out at the Infant Welfare Clinics, which have now increased in numbers...Each child attending receives orange juice, milk, Vitamin A and D concentrate and a sunbath, after being washed and 'groomed'."[14]

The work in the desert was generally recognised to be arduous in the extreme. The relentless sun, the loose sand, the frequent sand storms, all added to the difficulties facing relief workers. Personal equipment and even complete tents were occasionally prey to marauding Arabs, as carefully reconstructed tents made fine sails for Nile sailing boats.[15]

Not only the Arabs showed ingenuity. Somehow fabric, nails, wood, yarn and tools were found for the workshops established in the camps. The women spent hours at the camp sewing machine, making clothes for their children from the oddest of odds and ends. One former student remembers Elsie in the early 1960s describing in a lecture how the provision of good food to the women in the camp caused a crisis. All the women started to menstruate at once. There were few sanitary towels to be had, but one nappy each was allowed, and with this the women had to manage. Unfortunately, the women saw an opportunity to make some children's garments when the nappy was no longer needed, and so the next month saw a repetition of the crisis.[16]

Such anecdotes remained with Elsie throughout her life, and were drawn from the rich seam of humour that she found at Khatatba.

"There are many happy incidents I should like to report about these people, and maybe in a later report I'll have more time for the lighter side of Khatatba."[17]

The war was not changing Elsie's love of laughter. Yet she also treated the Yugoslavs in her care with respect and admiration for their sturdy independence. Perhaps their courage against all odds provided an example for her own rebellious stance against the establishment in years to come. The experiences she gained at Khatatba left a deep impression. Some twenty years later, she wrote:

"In almost all national groups, grief has certain 'permissive' actions. I well remember the way that grief was shown by the Yugoslav peasants, while refugees in Egypt, when death occurred. A shared waiting outside the hospital tent, a demand for photographs of the dead, - grief was open - all were permitted to join in, the young and the old. This form of demonstration is not unknown in many countries and, in this country, we need to understand grief and what open expression is acceptable. It is only by first understanding our own cultural patterns and then by using and understanding the differences of other human beings that we can begin to have full humanity."[18]

If Elsie occasionally failed to find the exact words to express her meaning, the general impression of her message is clear enough.

A further means of personal growth for Elsie was to be found among the other staff with whom she rubbed shoulders. One member of the medical team, Dr. Louise Fraser, committed to paper some clinical impressions based on the refugees at Khatatba. A handwritten copy of this document, dedicated with "Best love to Elsie Stephenson, the best little fraterniser in Yugoslavia", remains among Elsie's papers. The fact that Elsie received a copy suggests that she had shown an interest in a written report of this kind; the description of Elsie in the dedication is perhaps best left to the imagination.

Of great interest, with regard to Elsie's thought development, is the respect in which the writer holds the Yugoslav's customs, and her readiness to review the customs of British medical and nursing staff in the light of this experience.

"The Yugoslav refugees near Suez are living in large tents, several families to a tent. Their morale, cleanliness and cheerfulness are surprising, even to one who knew them during the last War. Many of these women have been in concentration camps under the Italians, others have had to wander through the woods and hills, to escape the Germans. All have, or have had, close relatives fighting with the Partisans under Tito, and many do not know the fate of their relatives."[19]

Dr. Fraser noted with approval how a Yugoslav baby was put to the breast as soon as the afterbirth was delivered, whereas in Britain the baby's sucking reflex died down during the first twenty-four hours of life, while the exhausted mother was regaining her strength.

"Our own nurses are inclined to regard regular breast feeding as the Law and Prophets. Even in the hot dry climate of Egypt, they proposed the four-hourly feed, (introduced to persuade the society lady to fit it in between social engagements)."

This doctor was prepared to learn from her patients, and noted how simply the refugees dealt with a problem that had exercised the minds of lecturers preparing staff for work with refugees:

"One of my patients boasted that she had always fed another child besides her own. A lecture on the feeding of refugee infants, which I heard in London, mentioned practically everything but wet-nursing. It is the first thing to try, where the child's own mother cannot feed it."[20]

Such influences fanned the flames of Elsie's growing passion for innovation, and for practice based on reason. At the same time, her contact with the Yugoslavs developed her admiration for rebels with a cause. Unfortunately, she also had a price to pay for her dedication to duty. After ten days' leave in Cairo at the end of July, she returned to the innoculations at Khatatba, and to the Labour Ward, so busy that, on occasion, she had to sleep there. On 7th September, conjunctivitis was reported. The infection spread rapidly, and within two days Elsie was treating 122 cases three times a day, as well as coping with a premature baby in her tent at night. A week later, the eye cases were slowly improving, but then Elsie woke up one morning with her left eye pouring pus.

19th September. *Very painful - could not sleep - got the girls to work then back to bed.*

20th September. *Roll on tomorrow so that I can get into hospital.*

21st September. *No sleep - refused to go in ambulance 9 a.m. - not told anything about it. Came in with Colonel Critchley 2 p.m. feeling lousy - thank God to be in bed.*

22nd September. *After + + dope managed to sleep eventually - the other eye infected - seem to have slept all day.*

Sedated with morphine, she slept for most of a week, but still her eyes were painful and she had difficulty seeing. Penicillin was prescribed two hourly - an early use of the then new wonder drug. By the beginning of October she was able to be out of bed for part of the day, and Colonel Critchley had arranged sick leave for her.

"An outbreak of purulent conjunctivitis during September was quickly brought under control by the setting up of an Eye Clinic where routine daily irrigation of the eye was instituted. This work was initiated and directed also by Sister

Stephenson, who unfortunately contracted the complaint towards the end of the epidemic, and reluctantly obeyed the order to go to 15th (S.) Hospital for treatment and rest. This epidemic began in the first week in September, and 270 patients were treated successfully. Two cases only required treatment in hospital."[21]

An eye problem had been the cause of her illness when she first arrived at El Shatt in March. Now exhaustion and overwork must certainly have contributed to the severity of her illness. According to the Principal Medical Officer's description of the conditions prevalent at Khatatba, it is a credit to the staff that only two people had to be admitted to hospital during this epidemic. Stifling weather, overcrowded tents, lack of soap and hot water, overdressing of children, reluctance to ventilate tents because of the sand blowing in; all of these conspired to produce ideal conditions for the spread of infection. As well as this, there was the problem of persuading mothers to feed their children a balanced diet. Bread and rice had been severely rationed during the Italian occupation of Yugoslavia, and so the mothers now believed these to be the most important ingredients of their children's diet. Protein deficiency was a serious risk, and children under six the most vulnerable. Milk was in such desperately short supply that women and children were rationed to 3.2 oz. per day, and men to 1 oz. per day. Mothers would breast feed as long as possible.

In mid October, 1944, Khatatba refugee camp was closed down. One group of mothers and children were moved to Tolumbat, the rest to El Shatt. Meanwhile Elsie was making the most of her enforced leave by visiting the Holy Land, in spite of persistent problems with her eyes. Although her departure from Khatatba had been more sudden than she might have hoped, the next phase of her war work promised even greater satisfaction.

Chapter 4

The Promised Land

Fear Not to Sow

On 4th June, 1944, the Allies had entered Rome. On 20th October, 1944, Belgrade was liberated. Thousands of Yugoslav refugees, women, children, orphans and tuberculosis victims, ragged and starving, had arrived in Italy. They came from Dalmatia where they had been scratching an existence in fields and caves. By November, 1944, sixty-two British Red Cross civilian relief personnel were tending these victims of the war.[1]

To go to Italy, or even better, Yugoslavia, and work with the same people she had come to admire and respect in Egypt, became Elsie's objective. Her admiration for the Yugoslavs had some interesting precedents in the history of British women. Elsie Inglis during the First World War fell in love with the rugged country (then Serbia) and its people.[2] Flora Sandes, like Elsie Stephenson, came from Suffolk, and joined the Serbian army as a soldier during the First World War. She fought and suffered along with the Serbs, rose through the ranks, and was called up again during the Second World War.[3] Her friend in Belgrade was Dr. Katherine MacPhail, a courageous Scottish doctor who went out to Yugoslavia with Elsie Inglis' Scottish Women's Hospital team in the First World War, and remained there, serving in medical units and running a children's hospital until she retired to St. Andrews, Scotland, where she died in 1974 at the age of eighty-six. Elsie Stephenson met Dr. MacPhail on several occasions in Yugoslavia, and later used to take an aged, but not subdued, Flora Sandes with her on her rounds back in Suffolk after the war.[4]

33

What was it about this country and these people that so enraptured these pioneering British women? No doubt the rugged beauty of the place cast its own spell, but also the sheer courage of the people fascinated these outstanding women. An American doctor, during the First World War, had been amazed by the courage he met:

"My word, ..., but I tell you these men are great. I feel so small beside them that I could hide myself. Pain! Suffering! You've not seen bravery until you've seen these men suffer. I'd take off a hand, an arm, or a leg - without anaesthetics, mind you - and will the fellow budge? - no, not an eyelid...Where this race of soldiers sprang from I don't pretend to know, but I tell you right now they are God's own men."[5]

In the refugee camp at Khatatba, Elsie had heard their songs and their death wails, admired their loyalty to Tito. Yet, ironically, without the war, the Partisans might never have found this sense of national cohesion. Since its formation as a state after the First World War, Yugoslavia had been torn by conflict between Serbs and Croats. Following the coup d'etat of March, 1941, a popular revolt against the Tripartite Agreement which would allow Germany to move troops across Yugoslav territory, Hitler declared the immediate invasion of Yugoslavia.[6]

By the time the Nazi planes left after the bombardment, Belgrade was a smoking ruin, and the country in a state of chaos. Thousands of men wandered about, some in the mountains, some picking up weapons. Between 1941 and 1945, in the continuing conflict between Communist and non-Communist guerillas, 600,000 people are thought to have been killed by fellow Slavs.

Tito, leader of the Communist guerillas, wanted an all-out popular revolt, a national liberation movement, and saw the war as an opportunity to bring the revolution about.

Mihailovic, leader of the Cetniks, was entirely reactionary, wanting the old order to prevail. In the early years of the war, Britain supported the Cetniks, but this did not prevent the Yugoslav resistance forces from enjoying a degree of success against the Germans in the summer of 1941.

Nazi reprisals were once more swift and horrifying. In October, 1941, for example, the entire male population of Kragujevac (about 5000 men over the age of 15 years) were shot in batches of 100 throughout one day. This same ill-fated town had seen the worst of the typhus epidemic during World War I, and Dr. Elsie Inglis had distinguished herself in the work she did to alleviate the suffering.[7]

Although the Nazis apparently quelled the rebellious Partisans in 1941, and the King and his ministers were exiled to London, Tito and his Partisans worked on doggedly, constantly short of food, living on nettles, herbs, beech leaves, sorrel and wild garlic. Gradually forming the Partisans into a regular military force, Tito fostered relations with the civilians. Any food taken was paid for, and plunder was not permitted. By November, 1943, Tito was able to set up a provisional government, and Britain supported the country with supplies.

Tito's supporters were fiercely proud of their achievements against all odds, and it was this great sense of purpose and bravery which affected Elsie Stephenson so profoundly. And so, when Khatatba closed in October, 1944, her move to Bari in Italy seemed the logical next step on her journey to the promised land. The crossing from North Africa to Italy was a hazardous affair towards the end of the war. When Bari, a key port in southern Italy, had been bombarded by Nazi planes in December, 1943, 17 Allied ships had been sunk, with more than 1000 casualties,[8] among them many nurses.

"Going over from North Africa to Italy was no joke. Several ships with Q.A.s* on board had only recently been sunk. The casualty rate among nursing personnel had not been low."[9]

Elsie is remembered as being the life and soul of the party crossing on the Ormond from North Africa to Taranto in Italy. At every opportunity, she joined the New Zealanders she had met in Egypt, and set her mind to such activities as organising a skipping competition. Even the captain joined in.[10]

Her diary is characteristically succinct on the subject:

18th November, 1944: *P.T. Not too fit. Sang Kiwi songs.*

20th November, 1944: *Taranto sighted. Ormond anchored 1.15 p.m. Waved goodbye to Kiwis - landed Taranto 2 p.m. Apples + + and roast chestnuts.*

22nd November, 1944: *Up 5.45 a.m. - luggage left 6 a.m. - breakfast 7 a.m. and left Taranto - crossed bay in rowing boats then on to train for Bari.*

Since September, 1944, the Allies had been planning a big push forward. The Eighth Army and the American Fifth Army had won ground around the Po delta and the town of Bologna respectively. It became clear, however, that the Allies would not be able to oust the Germans from Italy until the spring, such was the appalling state of the countryside as a result of flooding. The troops were exhausted, besides, and ammunition to support them was in short supply.[11]

The Joint War Organisation (J.W.O.) teams attached to the Eighth Army had been reinforced to meet the expected advance, and refugee camps were being prepared at road and rail heads from Ancona northwards. With the decision of the army to go into winter quarters, much reorganisation of

* *Queen Alexandra's Nursing Corps.*

J.W.O. personnel was also necessary. The British Red Cross, as part of the J.W.O., was primarily concerned with the large numbers of refugees pouring into the camps. With the onset of winter, accommodation problems became acute, and the two J.W.O. workers allocated to each camp were fully occupied with the distribution of food and clothing and finding useful occupation for the refugees.[12]

All of which may explain the confusion which met Elsie when she arrived in Bari. Her praise stopped at the palatial villa with lemon and orange groves where she stayed in San Spirito, and her diary reflects this.

23rd November, 1944: *General briefing at 10 a.m. - lunch - hitched into Bari, found N.Z. club. Hitched back to San Spirito - Mass meeting - a lot of dribble [sic].*

24th November, 1944: *Meeting...not too hopeful - wrote a letter to Red Cross re our opinion of work in an Italian refugee camp.*

Elsie's ambition was to go to Yugoslavia, and, having come this far, she was unwilling to accept any other occupation.

"With great expectations, I arrived in Italy on November 22, expecting to move on almost at once to Yugoslavia. This was not to be, as from November to January we waited in San Spirito, spirits soared one day and sank the next."[13] Until the end of the year, she spent her time sightseeing, visiting her friends at the New Zealand Hospital, where she indulged her weakness for Kiwi cake,[14] and taking Serbo Croat lessons.

On one memorable sightseeing trip in December, she met by chance her New Zealand friend Mac Sopp. Together they visited Naples, Capri (where Elsie drove a horse and cab), Sorrento, Amalfi, Pompeii and Rome. Elsie commented in her diary that Naples was "not as dirty as I expected."

What she expected is subject for conjecture. The situation in Naples had certainly been appalling for some time. When the American troops had first occupied Naples in October, 1943, they had found the population starving amid total devastation. Before leaving, the Nazis had apparently gone on a trail of destruction, looting and executing citizens. Food stocks were plundered or destroyed, as well as the city's water system. People were reduced to queuing at the outlet of the city's main sewer for their supply of water. The task of repairing the destruction, feeding the populace and preventing epidemics, was awesome. By the time Queen Alexandra nurses arrived early in 1944, following the advancing British army, the Catugno hospital lacked electric light and water. In January, typhus was devastating the civilian population, and volunteers were recruited to help stem the outbreak. In the hospital, three or four patients shared a bed; blankets and food were scarce; and patients, their mouths and eyes covered in sores, were shivering and starving. Italian nursing staff were in desperately short supply, and so the patients' basic needs were left unanswered.[15]

Elsie's diary records little of the horror that Italy had so recently endured.

8th December, 1944: *Naples raining. Spent morning looking round - not as dirty as I expected. Hitched to Pompeii. It must have been a wonderful city.*

9th December: *Arrangements broke down for Rome - got a lift in jeep. 6 in a jeep - packed like sardines - some of the places were completely gutted - a lovely run - rained a good deal.*

With hindsight, it seems strange that Elsie should have made so little of the destruction she saw in Italy. Perhaps such scenes were becoming part of her everyday experience, and therefore not worthy of comment. But also, her leanings were clearly towards action rather than reflection or analysis, particularly of the darker side of life.

On 6th January, 1945, she started work on Ward 13 of the 98th General Hospital in Bari, as waiting for transport to Yugoslavia seemed endless, and working there was "better than doing nothing," as she explained in a letter to Dame Emily Blair. Nursing Partisans in this surgical orthopaedic ward was useful from the point of view of learning the language, she felt, as well as occupying her time and keeping her skills fresh.

Ten thousand wounded Yugoslavs had been airlifted to hospitals in Italy when Britain began to supply Tito in 1943, and, while Elsie enjoyed the opportunity to nurse them, there were some ugly scenes between rival factions of patients. Partisans would refuse their food, suspecting the Cetniks of having poisoned it. Women Partisan patients were all supplied with hand grenades, and nurses were very wary of being misunderstood by these fiery patients. Partisans and Cetniks were repatriated separately, in order to avoid the risk of the Partisans dropping the Cetniks over the side of the ship on the way home.[16] Either Elsie was blissfully unaware of the tension between these rival groups, or she was fully conscious of the realities, but still beguiled by the Partisans' cause.

Although not a member of a political party, Elsie, now and throughout her life, responded to rebels with a cause. The Partisans were the most determined group of rebels she had met in her life, and from them she learned much about strength of purpose.

With her final goal in mind she spoke to Colonel Lewis and Colonel Neubauer, the Yugoslav Red Cross representatives, about working in Yugoslavia. Finally on 12th February, 1945, the company was ordered to assemble. Stores which had previously gone to the Egyptian refugee camps were redirected to Yugoslavia, and the British Red Cross stores in Bari supplied equipment to help with setting up a children's hospital.

On 7th March, she was saying goodbye to her friends at San Spirito, preparing for her departure from Bari to Ljubljana. "Thursday, March 8 was the great day, at last after one year and two months, the promised land was reached."[17]

Seasickness prevented her appreciating the realisation of her ambition until she was travelling by jeep, prone to punctures, from Split to Dubrovnik, on 13th March.

Elsie's report on this first venture into Yugoslavia - a later newspaper report claims she was the first British nurse to go into Yugoslavia after the war[18] - reflects her excitement. As she writes to Dame Emily Blair,

"We arrived in Dubrovnik on March 13 after a tiring yet thrilling journey by jeep. The countryside is magnificent and the scenery all I had ever imagined and the flowers beautiful. The Germans had gutted several small villages, yet the peasants were working in the patches of land; it was indeed heartening to see the activity everywhere and the unbelievable cleanliness."

In her diary, she was much more brief: "A wonderful run, through the mountains, houses gutted - snow-capped mountains - glimpses of the sea." Her first impressions, after the wonder of the scenery, were of cleanliness, good order, and the loveliness of Dubrovnik. Oddly, instead of the expected glow of satisfaction on having attained her goal, she was hit by homesickness. "Went round hospital in morning - very, very clean - chilly night - oh to be home," she reports for 16th March, 1945. Until mid April, she worked in schools, hospitals, and the Polyclinic. The war was proceeding all around. On 6th April, Sarajevo fell to the Allies, and on 9th April, the Fifth Army entered Milan. Roosevelt died on 13th April, and the Allies reeled from the untimely loss. Elsie was miserable:

13th April, 1945:...*Very cold and altogether very tired and fed up - to bed early."*

The main highlight in these days was to go on board ship at Dubrovnik to have a bath.

On April 15th, she was detailed to accompany Colonel Gordon, who had been ill in Yugoslavia for several weeks, back to hospital in Bari. When she returned to Yugoslavia, the situation was grimmer than before. Elsie worked at the Polyclinic from the end of April until the end of May. Early in May however she was confined to bed with a raised temperature, when the bells began to ring, and the guns to fire in celebration. Germany had surrendered.

8th May, 1945: *Surrender of Germany heard over wireless by Churchill at 2 p.m. Feeling awful - not up to hear King speak - still running a temperature. Wonder how things are at home.*

Once restored to health, it was possible to admit to enjoying life again.

19th May, 1945: *A glorious day - in and out of the sea + + - washed my hair - a grand post - 15 letters - lunch and supper in the garden.*

A few days later, she spent a memorable day by the sea with some of the children from the Children's Home, and this appears in her Report on Yugoslavia for March-June of 1945:

"We left the old harbour at Dubrovnik at 7 a.m. all packed into one small boat, one Sister and the boatsman rowing. We had not been at sea half an hour when a bora blew up and ere long everyone was sick. I was kept busy preventing anyone from falling overboard. After three hours at sea, we arrived at a glorious little port on the Adriatic called Mlini, all our troubles were forgotten over lunch and bathing. At 6 p.m. we very reluctantly said goodbye and piled into the wee boat again. Tears were shed at the thought of more seasickness, but we arrived without trouble at 9 o'clock, tired but very happy."

Elsie's work at the Polyclinic was brightened by the arrival of the occasional ship in port, bringing letters and parcels from home, and treats like new potatoes. Yugoslavia in early summer, as later tourists came to realise, was a glorious place to be.

Work in the Polyclinic entailed long hours, but was not otherwise strenuous, and the contacts made there led to mutual trust and respect. The Yugoslav Red Cross had plans in hand to open up small hospitals all down the coast, and Dr. Novakovic of the Public Health Department, Dubrovnik, suggested that Elsie could supervise the work and help to train their nurses and aides. Understandably, she was to feel deeply aggrieved when all these good relationships were upset. Now and again she had commented that things were not too good in Yugoslavia. The blow was struck on 31st May, when her diary entry records: "Bad news. To stop work."

The reason for the abrupt cessation of her work in Yugoslavia appears to have been general confusion over the respective roles of the Red Cross and U.N.R.R.A. at this sensitive stage. Elsie wrote in her Report on Yugoslavia, the following:

"On my return to Yugoslavia [after accompanying Colonel Gordon to Italy] I was asked by Dr. Novakovic, Public Health Department, and head of Yugoslav Red Cross in Dubrovnik to obtain a written assignment for me to be turned over to them from my immediate chief. This I obtained from Major Garfield. I was then able to continue my work in the Polyclinic. I was then asked to cease work by ...U.N.R.R.A., unless I had written permission from Belgrade to carry on. After discussing this with Dr. Novakovic and he with his committee, I was requested to stop working. This decision was, I am sure, due to the forcing of their hand, regarding a reply from Belgrade."

The official war history of the British Red Cross hints at the difficulties without elaborating on their cause:

"The British Red Cross had teams standing by in Egypt and Italy to assist in civilian relief services in Yugoslavia. Circumstances which it was not within its power to control prevented the teams being so used...Three British Red Cross members only accompanied the relief personnel who worked in Yugoslavia under the auspices of U.N.R.R.A."[19]

Elsie felt very bitter, and complained to every possible authority. Eventually, a signal came through permitting personnel to resume work, but Elsie felt too much damage had been done to relationships to make this feasible.

"I feel very strongly that if we had been able to go into Yugoslavia as British Red Cross only, we should have done a good job. A representative should have been sent to Belgrade and arrangements made for work. I still feel that if this was done we should then be able to work with the Yugoslavs...they need us so badly...

Kindness and hospitality was shown me both by the Partisans and the Civilians, and my one regret is that my hand was not free. If only I had been able to work on my own I could have done a real job worthy of the British Red Cross. My great wish is to return at a later date to those unfortunate yet wonderful people. Our withdrawal was a great blow to them, for they understood and trusted the British Red Cross."[20]

The abrupt cessation of Elsie's work in Yugoslavia appears to have been caused by the political situation, and not by any failure of good will on the part of U.N.R.R.A., an organisation which had brought "a message of hope...to millions of hapless victims of war's ruthless desolation."[21] In June she began saying her goodbyes.

Tuesday, 12th June, 1945: *A heavenly day. This a.m. orders to move on Thursday - very very sad - said goodbye to Dr. MacPhail. A wonderful day - yet one of the saddest we could have.*

The return journey on the French Eridan went smoothly. On arrival in Bari, Elsie admitted to her diary that it was wonderful to have real comfort again. Her task from now until mid October involved planning refugee camp welfare services in Italy. Characteristically, she did not, however, lose sight of the basics:

31st July l945: *Bought nit combs.*

Her itinerary around Italy seems humanly impossible. She went from Bari to Naples, to Rome, to Forli, to Ancona, to Fano, to Bologna, to Mantua, Verona and Lake Garda, through the Brenner Pass to Innsbruck, back to Milan, Ancona, Fano, Senigallia, Bari, where there was a brief hope of going on leave. Instead, she continued attending to stores, training her successor, being eaten alive by mosquitoes and bugs. From 28th September until 16th October, she covered Milan, Venice, Trieste, Senigallia, Rome, Sorrento and Capri, presumably on a final tour of inspection of the refugee camps before returning home.

It is easy to appreciate that she fully deserved the testimonial written by a U.S. Army Lieutenant Colonel in September, 1945:

"She has sought and obtained by every possible means, clothing, shoes, medical supplies, supplies for camp sewing classes, for kindergartens, and has been alert to obtain materials for other uses outside her own field. She is intelligent, resourceful, keen, able to a high degree; has been able to get things done, has been quite tireless in driving about the large territory she had to cover; has achieved excellent results; has been far more than satisfactory.

In organising the medical, hospital and public health services in the newly established refugee camps, she has in my opinion shown administrative and organising ability and judgment. I have found her work highly useful, her judgment, her initiative and intelligence excellent, her energy and faithfulness first rate."

For her contribution to the welfare services during World War II, Elsie received the Italian Star, the 1939-45 Star, the Defence Medal, and was made a Serving Sister of the Order of St. John of Jerusalem.

It seems fair to say that Elsie was not seeking honours when she gave her whole being to the work in hand during the war. It was simply in her nature to live life to the full and to do her utmost for those in need. Her disappointment over Yugoslavia firmly behind her, she had thrown herself into the work in Italian refugee camps.

When in 1967, she had the chance to return to Yugoslavia and see what progress had been made, she admitted to shedding a few tears at the stirring of old memories.[22]

Chapter 5

Putting the Lid Back On

Fear Not to Sow

Although the war was over, the suffering continued. Red Cross workers were involved in civilian relief work wherever there was destitution, administering relief on an unprecedented scale in Europe, as vast numbers of displaced persons wandered across Germany. Six units from the British Red Cross Commission were sent to Belsen in April, 1945, and in May, Mobile Hospital No. 1 was transferred from the Rhine to Belsen. Civilian relief work in Germany included work in camps for displaced persons and for German refugees in the British zone, as well as care of tuberculosis patients, general relief, welfare work, and actual nursing.[1]

When Elsie joined Mobile Hospital No. 5, B.R.C.S. Civilian Relief, at Bad Münder in North Germany, in November, 1945, she was closer than ever to the effects of the fighting and cruelty of the past six years. She had some regrets about leaving home again, especially as her brother Harry had come home from the war during her last night before leaving for Germany.

15th November, 1945: *Sad at leaving - trust Mother will keep well.*

After a week of waiting at transit hostels, interspersed with bouts of travelling by train, boat and ambulance, she finally reached Bad Munder in late November.

23rd November, 1945: *Left for Bad Münder - arrived 5 p.m.- a very attractive spot and a comfortable house - worried if O.K. to take over.*

26th November: *Snowing - really taking hold - untold problems. Worked hard all day. German evening - to bed late, very tired.*

News of the findings at Belsen were already reverberating throughout the world by the time Elsie set foot in Germany. She would have heard of the conditions found there by the first relief team: the stench; the shelves where inmates lay five abreast in a space unfit for one; corpses lying uncovered on the ground among rotten straw and excreta; people no more than degraded parcels of bones over which the lice played.

Ailments from which these wretches suffered included every scourge known to mankind - typhus, typhoid, septicaemia, gonorrhoea, dysentery, diphtheria, erysipelas, broncho-pneumonia. Moreover, the effects of famine were manifest in the high incidence of oedema, gingivitis, pellagra, extreme emaciation, profound lassitude.

Added to all this, the Nazi regime had left its victims in utter mental despair. They hid the supplies brought to them by the Red Cross under their mattresses for fear that the Nazis would take them away, or worse, shoot the possessor. When clothes were finally obtained for the babies who had till then been wrapped in tissue paper in the maternity wards, the mothers bartered them for food.[2]

Elsie could, therefore, be excused her apprehension when she took up her post as Senior Sister at Bad Munder. The hospital building had been used during the war as a German military hospital, and lay in beautiful hilly country halfway between Bremen and Hameln. Once German patients had been transferred to other hospitals, Mobile Hospital No. 5 began admitting displaced persons, some of whom had spent the war as prisoners working on German farms and estates, or in factories or quarries, while others had been in concentration camps.

One can only begin to imagine the "untold problems" Elsie mentioned in her diary. Many of the patients in the hospital were broken people, in spirit, in mind, in body. The staff were multi-national. Some of the doctors and nurses were German, and the patients' unwillingness to have dealings with them can well be understood. Elsie did not make any further entries in her diary during the Bad Munder period, and so the story is left to those who still remember her work. Rose van den Berg was a nurse there:

"However mixed a company we were, a very pleasant atmosphere existed and everyone [was] very keen to do the job."[3]

Although the Mobile Hospital carried with it equipment for about 50 patients, the equipment already in the building was used at Bad Munder. There were no children's beds, however, and so Elsie had some made by a local carpenter. Although most of the patients were Polish, there were also Russians, Latvians, Lithuanians, Estonians and stateless people. Over 100 were men, about 40 women and 20 children.

"The language was quite a problem, sometimes one needed two interpreters, three if one did not understand German. Many of the patients knew a little German but [were] not always willing to speak it as they had no kind feelings towards anything German."[4]

Wincenty Tylmanowski, with his knowledge of English and German, was an asset to the hospital in his role as Polish liaison officer. He remembers the sensitive diplomacy required of the hospital management.

"The most important duty for the British personnel was to create by all means a friendly atmosphere between the Germans and the patients. Without...reciprocal confidence the proper work of the hospital was practically impossible...There were pretty hard days in the hospital at the beginning but later...the patients as well as the staff were feeling like one big family."5

Patients were kept busy making whatever they could with obtainable materials, and the list of articles completed in the month of February included "17 embroidered boleros, 32 shirts, 25 jumpers, 16 pullovers, 12 pairs children's slippers, 10 toys, 6 dolls, 4 pairs socks, l leather snapshot album, l rug, 3 Polish badges."6 With an eye to the future, Elsie planned to teach nursing to the women and girls so that they could eventually take over the care of their fellow patients.

A wood carving class was started, and there were twice weekly film shows, as well as English lessons, begun at Elsie's suggestion and taught by one of the English V.A.D.s (Voluntary Aid Detachment). For the children, housed in a separate building,in another former hilltop hotel, Elsie arranged classes taught by two of the V.A.D.s. Weather permitting, lessons were conducted outside in the field. Mobile Hospital No. 5 staff were housed in two buildings near the hospital.

"Mealtimes were pleasant times and many a witty and lively conversation and discussion was heard. When not at work, we enjoyed walking in the beautiful hills and woods around us or spent many pleasant hours together in the house. We were fortunate to have a ping-pong table, a wireless set and gramophone...

Quite often we used to go back to the hospital in the evening, to the main hall, where the up-patients had a hot drink before going to bed and where informal dances were held for patients and staff. How well Elsie could dance the Polish polka."7

Constant activity for the patients was deliberate policy. All of the patients were emotionally disturbed to some extent by their wartime experiences, and some were mentally ill. Many of the Polish male patients had been sent to

Germany after having been taken prisoner during the Polish revolt, and appalling memories of their treatment were still fresh in their minds. Rose van den Berg recalls one day in particular when the atmosphere was taut.

"I overtook Elsie who had stopped a patient leaving the hospital grounds with a parcel under his arm. She asked him to open it, suspecting that hospital property was being taken away to be bartered for beer or something more potent. Her suspicion proved to be true - unpleasant for both parties. One had to be on the alert always as the most impossible could be possible here. Tension could grow enormously in no time about nothing. So one day when the patients received jam instead of marmalade they expected to have, it came to an outbreak...

During that day full of discontent and turmoil when feelings ran so high that, as far as possible, everybody was ordered out of sight for safety's sake, I well remember seeing Elsie and Lt. Tylmanowski (the Polish liaison officer) in the centre of the hall with a crowd of angry patients around them - talking and interpreting and talking again. I do not know what Elsie thought or felt at that moment, but she did not show anything. Peace returned but for a short time we had a few British soldiers on guard at the hospital."

Christmas, 1946, was "both a joy and a shock" to the patients according to Miss van den Berg.

"For some of the patients the emotion was too great; tall, big men fainted, overcome by their memories...As soon as they could sit or stand they pleaded with the doctor to be allowed to go back to the Christmas celebrations. It was unforgettable for all of us."

Wincenty Tylmonowski remembers how Elsie tried to make Christmas Eve a traditionally Polish occasion. They sang Polish songs, and ate Polish food.

"During the service I have been playing the organ and we were singing Polish Christmas songs. Some patients took part in the service on stretchers...I think I shall say the truth that during this evening lots of us had tears in eyes. These were the tears of happiness that we could do something for the luckless ill people."8

The lighter side of life was not neglected. Elsie took the opportunity to try skiing with Daisy Stroinski, the hospital interpreter. As the evenings were the only free time available for skiing lessons, they set forth, Elsie on Daisy's sister's skis, and each carrying a lamp borrowed from Daisy's father. The pair had much fun, and Elsie had the chance to revitalise her spirits.9

Such moments of recreation did not prevent the patients from seeing Elsie as the devoted nurse, always on hand when needed. Wincenty Tylmanowski recalls that she visited every room to say goodnight to the patients before going off duty. She was equally attentive to the bedbound patients, most of whom died. "I can assure you that there hasn't been a dying patient who hasn't been seen by Elsie in the last moment of his life."

When a Polish patient died, Wincenty Tylmanowski covered the coffin with the Polish flag.

"I shall never forget the moment as Elsie approached me and covered the coffin beside the Polish flag with the British one. She did this on every funeral. When I asked Elsie why...she answered: 'We owed the Poles very much during the last war and from the time my fatherland declared war on Hitler we have been allies for death and life'." [10]

Her popularity with the patients can be judged by the enormous birthday card, hand painted and written in Polish, which she received from the Bad Münder patients on 22nd January, 1946, her thirtieth birthday.

Being Elsie, and with the training she had, she must have thought of the homes to which her patients hoped eventually to return. There could be no doubt that more anguish awaited the lucky ones who would reach home. Eye witnesses were describing the grey tide of misery slowly seeping over the river Oder to the west, the Germans retreating away from the area now occupied by the Poles.

Those who had seen them were haunted by the dim, hungry eyes of these ragged skeletons, many of them children, wandering from village to village begging for a crust of bread. Now and again the pitiful line would stop to bury a child or an old man who had died along the way. Then the march would continue; the search for food and lodgings would trail in vain from door to door, village to village. No one had food or rooms to give them. The army of survivors grew smaller and smaller as the youngest children, the old people, and those weakened by disease succumbed and died by the roadside. The living envied those who had found peace, and could be heard crying, "Send us an atom bomb!" as they wandered along the road to nowhere.[11]

Mecklenburg, Brandenburg and Saxony were worst affected, as they filled to overflowing with evacuees from East Germany and the zones occupied by the Poles and Czechs. The Potsdam declaration had forbidden compulsory evacuation by the Poles, but nonetheless, the latter could not resist the opportunity to wreak their vengeance. They appropriated goods and land belonging to Germans, abolished German currency and withheld food. Even in peace time it would have been difficult to feed the estimated 18 million people thronging into the area around Saxony. Now that the harvest had been seized by the Russians, and half the houses were destroyed, it looked as if ten million Germans would be dead by the spring of 1946.

Famine was the great killer. The dead bodies were swollen with dropsy. Potatoes were the only food for three-quarters of the population of Brandenburg and mothers would chew cooked potatoes and push the pap into the mouths of their infants in the hope of keeping them alive. People were so weakened by hunger that they often died of typhoid inoculations, given to protect them, in the British and American zones of Berlin.

In Eastern Germany, it was reported that 10,000 children were found wandering about without parents, scavenging for food. Because of the lack of milk (Frankfurt on the Oder, for instance, had 45,000 inhabitants and only 15 cows) and because the mothers were too weak to nurse their babies, most young children could not survive. Thousands of refugees collected at the stations, and trains would transport them on such futile journeys as Mecklenburg to Berlin, Berlin to Saxony, Saxony to Thuringen, and Thuringen back to Mecklenburg.

Reports from the areas around Berlin claimed that what little food there was was now being taken to the capital, where the eyes of the world were focussed. In the Arnswald region, almost all infants died, and 80 per cent of women over thirteen years were suffering from venereal diseases. In Gotenhafen, German orphans were being sold for ten zloty each, and stories were told of Germans being robbed on trains. One eye witness claimed to have seen a Polish soldier on a train tear a German woman's infant from her and throw the child out of the carriage window.[12]

Relief workers battled on against impossible odds. In a fever hospital south of Berlin, two elderly nurses and some untrained domestics were looking after 150 patients, with equipment totalling two clinical thermometers and one bedpan; no bed clothes, no disinfectant, soap or instruments. Patients brought their own bed linen, which their family laundered. Often the family would then fall ill with typhoid, and they too would have to be admitted to the hospital.

Those patients from Bad Münder who recovered and were repatriated often found their homes in ruin, their families split up, some dead, and a life which would never be the same again. Wincenty Tylmanowski longed to be repatriated with the others, but his linguistic skills were a scarce commodity. He was persuaded to remain in Germany with the Polish Red Cross, helping to trace displaced persons and reunite Polish families, until 1950. Then at last he was able to return to his diminished family in Poland and take up what was left of normal life again. He continued to keep in touch with Elsie.[13]

"Elsie did her best to help the patients in their distress, lighten them in their sufferings and their hankering for their fatherland. She will never be forgotten by all who knew her...We Poles shall always remember Elsie as the most sincere friend of us and our country." [14]

The post war world had entered into a new era, about which, in 1944, Field Marshall Smuts had uttered some chilling words:

"We are now about to enter upon a new chapter in the history of mankind. We should thank God for Hitler. He has done a great service to the world. He has brought us back to a realisation of brutal facts. He has got us away from ideals and rhetoric. Facts are the only thing that matter. Hitler has shown that Hell is still here on Earth. He has, in fact, taken the lid off Hell, and we have all looked into it. That is his service to the human race."*15*

Elsie's work, like that of all other relief workers at that time, was to put the lid back on Hell and to help people live normal lives again. A few years later, at the Red Cross Conference in Stockholm, Lord Woolton spoke of the wartime and post-war contribution of health, nursing and relief workers:

"These people are among the world's greatest experts. Their motives are of the highest, and fortunately their technical skills match their humanitarian desires."[16]

Chapter 6

Post-War in Berlin

Fear Not to Sow

Health visiting had brought out the health educator in Elsie. Work in the camps at Khatatba and in Italy had reinforced her belief in the effectiveness of simple preventive measures in fostering health and vitality. Now she was to find herself in one of the most depressed and complex areas after the war, when the British Red Cross asked her to take part in a Child Welfare Team in Berlin.

Lady Falmouth of the B.R.C.S. had toured Germany and Austria for six weeks during November and December, 1945, to assess the conditions of German and Austrian people living in the British zones. The situation was so appalling that relief teams were recruited to undertake welfare work among German people. Women and children were to be the focus of care, but the whole welfare system needed to be reorganised along "non-Nazi" lines. [1]

The Chairman of Civilian Relief Overseas wrote to express satisfaction at Elsie's appointment:

"Pleased to hear from Vlotho that you have accepted a post in the nutrition team to Berlin. It is a great relief to our minds, for we are most anxious to get the right person for this team which should do most important and valuable work.

I hear too that you have generously put off your leave in order to start. This is very good of you as I know you have been looking forward to it." [2]

She did manage a brief visit to Newmarket, when her diary records a morning at home with mother, and chicken for dinner. After her experiences in Egypt and Europe, this must have been a rare taste of homeliness for Elsie.

Berlin at this stage was the focus of a multitude of complex repercussions from the war. Most evident was the shortage of food, but any solution to the problem was threatened by the atmosphere of bitterness and suspicion between the four occupying forces and the defeated Germans.

The temptation to humiliate the German population was, in many cases, irresistible. In Silesia, for instance, Germans, who had no ration cards of their own, were forced to beg for bread from the occupying Russians. Five truck loads of food sent from Britain for the starving Germans between December, 1945 and February, 1946 were intercepted by the Poles.[3]

Elsie had only recently sent copies of photographs of Belsen to friends in New Zealand. She had also witnessed the physical and mental effects of Nazi treatment of the people she nursed at Bad Münder. To find compassion for the 'race' responsible for such atrocities must have taxed the most charitable of souls, but that was precisely what was expected of the Child Welfare Team.

Young people represented the one flicker of hope in the whole situation. The children were innocent, and the future was theirs, and so one could throw oneself wholeheartedly into working for their well-being, no matter what their fathers had done. Yet even that small flame was still hedged around by the all-embracing Nazi plan for the world. If Elsie had seen how much good could be done by an efficient health plan for a community, she was about to learn, in Berlin, how much a corrupt leadership had used the nation's health to its own ends.

The German welfare system was still under the shadow of an organisation aimed at producing a carefully selected race of "nobility", free from genetic flaws, and safeguarded from dangerous infections. To this end, the Nazi regime had carried out its task with ruthless efficiency, and Elsie was often to see the disastrous effects of state control of health in the weeks to come.

For those of the chosen race, disease elimination had been frighteningly efficient. Any outbreak of a dangerous disease among the Aryan population had immediately been reported to the central authority, and at selected research centres, the disease had been diagnosed, vaccines and medicines released on the spot, hospital beds ruthlessly cleared for the isolation of the patient or carrier, and the danger stamped out before it could spread. The lessons of World War I, where weary and undernourished bodies fell prey to malaria, louse-borne typhus, influenza, tuberculosis and venereal disease had not been lost on the Nazis, and so sanitary defence had formed an integral part of rearmament.

Health for the Nazi regime had meant not only freedom from disease but also fertility and racial improvement. Every imaginable means of science and legislation had been used to promote the birth rate of the Aryan population, with one billion Reichsmark spent to this end each year.

The other side of the coin had been the elimination of undesirable strains, achieved by such means as sterilisation, abortion, prohibition from marrying and segregation from the German "race". The concentration camps had been seen by the authorities as carrying out valuable work in the improvement of the race. While maintaining a rising birth rate during the war years, the Nazi regime had carried out in excess of 100,000 compulsory abortions and sterilisations, and sent millions of "racial and genetic" enemies to their death.[4]

Berlin in that first year after the war was a frightening place to be, with looting and sacking of the city reportedly creating more terror among the population than the bombing.

Agencies like the Society of Friends, anxious to build bridges between warring factions, urged friendly contacts between the four powers.[5]

It must have been difficult to envisage any positive course of action to improve the situation in Berlin in even the smallest way. The Child Welfare Team had to tread warily and record its findings accurately. During the project, 11 infant welfare clinics, 4 kindergartens, 12 schools, 16 central kitchens, 10 children's homes and orphanages, 4 day nurseries, 3 hospitals, 3 refugee camps and 19 individual homes were visited.[6]

These visits were recorded in notes, the details of which often summon up haunting pictures of living conditions. Typically, whole families would be living on onions and carrots. One home visitor found a mother with her five children, aged from eight months to twelve years, living in a two-roomed top flat.

"Three children have school meals but she said she could not let them go on as there were not enough coupons left. No food in the house till Monday except one tin condensed milk. Monday new ration period. Husband prisoner in France. Been in Berlin since 1930. Has no firewood, had arranged to have some but couldn't leave home to get it."[7]

Another report describes how a grandfather, his daughter, and her two children aged two and four, were living in modest comfort in a small bungalow constructed on open ground from salvage material. The lavatory was a bucket in the garden. Already the grandfather had sown seeds, and he was improving conditions daily for his family.

Expectant and nursing mothers were generally short of rations, with the result that young mothers tended to be weak and emaciated. Pregnant women missed out on the health education recognised by the team to be so important for them, for the simple reason that any leaflets available in ante-natal clinic still referred to Nazi institutions. Plenty of maternity beds were available in hospitals, but few people wanted them, since ration books had to be surrendered on admission to hospital. Food shortages were producing a general tendency to rickets.

Institutions visited by the team seemed to be suffering from a peculiar loss of drive and purpose, exemplified by the lack of instruction available in welfare centres, the poor ventilation and overheating in schools, hospitals and kindergartens. The team's report described "a great lack of initiative amounting almost to inertia at a time when educational propaganda is so greatly needed."

The shadow of the Nazi system still dominated decision-making in some areas. In one infant welfare centre, for instance, lists of children to receive Swedish food parcels had been made out according to Nazi party criteria. Health workers had to produce new lists, taking account of the real needs of children. In refugee camps, a similar failure to define the needy resulted in cod liver oil and vitamins being handed out indiscriminately. The fall of the Nazis had also left the youth of Germany with no unifying ideal to follow, so that their needs included not only more food, but also inspired leadership to give them a sense of purpose in life. Problems facing the Medical Officers of Health for Berlin and Charlottenburg ranged from skin eruptions caused by lack of soap to wash babies' napkins, to the lack of hospital beds for tuberculosis patients, since permission could not be obtained to send patients to the sanatorium which was in the Russian zone.

Hardly surprising, in this atmosphere, that the final report of the Child Welfare Team expressed a degree of dissatisfaction with its achievements during ten weeks in Berlin. They felt they had been hampered by the mistrust of the retiring Director of Public Health and the need to obtain agreement from all the four occupying powers to any of their proposals. Individual contacts such as they had achieved over the ten weeks could only produce limited results, they felt, and much more health propaganda was the only way forward.

Non-political propaganda, as recommended by the team, should take the form of nutritional education for doctors, nurses, teachers and housewives, using newspapers and radio for publicity, and general health education for health workers on the value of fresh air indoors. (It is fascinating that the value of fresh air was still stressed as much then as it had been in the days of Florence Nightingale's hospital reforms.) The team further recommended a visit from a British expert from one of the schools of social science to stimulate modern thought in health and welfare workers. This may well have been Elsie's first encounter with the discipline of social science.

Working with the Child Welfare Team, though disturbing and frustrating, provided Elsie with much food for thought. Man's continuing inhumanity to man, as seen in the vengeance and the petty-mindedness of Berlin in 1946, cannot have been an edifying experience. She drew strength once more from the impartial role of the Red Cross, and other caring agencies she met, such as the Society of Friends. The team's recommendations demonstrate how much all members, including Elsie, continued to believe in the importance of health education as a means of extricating a defeated populace from apathy and further degradation. Besides reinforcing this basic belief, the experience proved to the team the importance of keeping good records, in order to assess the health of a community. The potential value of social science as a discipline was recognised, and may have influenced Elsie's later leanings towards this relatively new science.

With the benefit of hindsight, Elsie delivered a lecture in 1960, drawing on this experience to demonstrate the value of health education for child welfare.

"During the Second World War, the mass movement of children, problems of deprivation, feeding and maintenance of health were studied closely...Radio, schools, voluntary organisations were all used, with the help of the public health nurse, to encourage people to accept the preventive aids for their children, e.g. diphtheria immunisation. The result was a standard of health far higher than the previous national average."[8]

Chapter 7

The Door of Opportunity

Fear Not to Sow

Elsie was awarded a Florence Nightingale International Foundation Scholarship in 1946, to study Advanced Public Health Administration at Toronto University. This wonderful opportunity came just at a time when, although her enthusiasm for nursing was in no way abated, she was sorely in need of a chance to think, to put into perspective what she had experienced during and after the war, and to make plans for the future.

This was an interesting time to win the scholarship, since the Florence Nightingale International Foundation (F.N.I.F.) was then working out is post-war policy, and recognising that changes were needed, not only in its organisation, but also its educational policies. Mary Adelaide Nutting had proposed the F.N.I.F.

"to form an international center for study and research in nursing and the kindred problems of hospitals and public health, upon which Miss Nightingale's mind had played with such amazing power and originality."[1]

Until the war, scholarship holders had studied together at 15, Manchester Square in London, but as the building had been totally destroyed by bombs, students were being sent to study abroad in any country deemed suitable by the Foundation's Education Committee or the National Committee of the country concerned.[2] Eileen Rees had won her scholarship in 1939, but was unable to take it up because of the war, and so she and Elsie set sail together from Southampton, among a large contingent of Canadian war

65

brides, on the last voyage of the Queen Mary as a war transport.

From the moment they landed in Canada, the atmosphere was of fun and camaraderie. A band turned out at the quay at Halifax to play Wagner's *Wedding March* for the brides on board. On the train from Halifax to Toronto, the driver recognised that Elsie and Eileen were "from Blighty" by the colour of their stockings, and invited them to sit up front beside him. He let Elsie drive for 150 miles, and stopped the train and waited while they went to buy ice cream. The weight of the responsibility of wartime nursing had dropped from their shoulders, and they were students.

Being students did, however, mean that they had very little spare cash to do justice to this opportunity to see the New World. They quickly set up the "Rocky Mountain Fund", raised from the proceeds of babysitting, to finance their projected visit to the west coast. Home for the year was the attic of a French Canadian family.[3]

As another means of increasing their income and enriching their experience, they approached the Canadian Red Cross to inquire about possible relief work during vacations. Christmas, therefore, found Elsie relieving the Matron of the Red Cross Outpost Station at Lions Head, Ontario. Amid increasingly heavy snowfalls, she attended district cases by sleigh, and even made the newspapers, when she delivered her two hundredth baby in the hospital at Lions Head, no doctor being able to penetrate the snowdrifts.

The international contacts made during this year in Canada were invaluable. As part of the international group in the University School of Nursing, Elsie and Eileen made friends with Rockefeller students from Norway, Sweden, Denmark, Finland, Belgium, Greece, Yugoslavia, Ecuador, Chile, India and U.S.A. and Red Cross students from India, all registered nurses with a wide variety of experience.[4]

Established in the University of Toronto in 1920, to train nurses in the newly developing field of public health, the Department of Public Health Nursing had, in 1942, initiated a programme leading to the degree of Bachelor of Science in Nursing, with an emphasis on integrating the preventive and curative aspects of nursing.[5] Learning about this course was a revelation to Elsie and Eileen. Like many others, they were acutely aware of the problems inherent in the British system of nurse education, based as it was on the apprenticeship system, but in reality relying heavily on student nurses to staff the wards, often at the expense of their own education. The Toronto University undergraduate programme covered five university years, during which students entered into normal university life, studying whichever subjects they chose, while also receiving a complete theoretical and practical nurse training. As well as gaining experience in general wards, students were affiliated to specialist hospitals for paediatrics, obstetrics, contagious diseases, psychiatric nursing and dietetics. Throughout the training, students were encouraged to concentrate on positive health and to view the patient as a whole person. It is interesting to note the similarities between this course and the integrated degree course which Elsie would later pioneer at Edinburgh University.

Another experimental course about to begin in Ontario attracted their attention. By awarding student nurses full student status and freeing them from unnecessary repetitive tasks, it intended to reduce the length of nurse training while in no way diminishing the quality. Public health instruction in this course too would emphasise total health care for the individual, the family and the whole of society.

The underlying principles of these courses supported and expanded the lines of thought Elsie was beginning to develop from her own training experience and personal philosophy.

The nurse was seen as a thinker as well as a doer, and this implied that the nurse should be provided with the best education possible. The aim was to provide opportunities for problem-solving, to develop initiative, resourcefulness, good judgment, self confidence and independence. As a thinker, the nurse must inevitably be aware of the causes of ill health, and therefore be prepared to promote positive health and prevention of disease. The nursing role, therefore, should entail looking at the patient as a whole person, and encouraging all-round health, just as Elsie had placed as much emphasis on occupational therapy as she had on drug therapy in her work with refugees and displaced persons.

Here in Toronto, the whole picture was coming together for Elsie, and the words of Charles Singer, quoted by policy makers, bore out what she had seen for herself in the refugee camps at Khatatba:

"It may reasonably be doubted whether all modern medical and surgical advances put together - apart from preventive medicine and infant hygiene - have saved as many lives as the reform of nursing."[6]

She was introduced to the concept of how recent advances in human knowledge necessitated advances in nursing education and practice. The recently collected knowledge of the structure of human society, social science, was affecting nurse teaching most profoundly.

"Where we saw a confused mass of individuals related to each other in very imperfectly understood ways now there is being revealed to us - as a tissue comes clear under a microscope - an orderly pattern of human living. From our own special standpoint we see our patients no longer as bodies in bed, but as dynamic persons belonging to numerous social groups, persons with pasts and futures who may indeed suffer harm from hospitalisation if we fail to recognise their social and personal problems as well as their diseases."[7]

Elsie had been part of the team which recommended a social science expert to help solve the problems for child welfare in Berlin. Here, she was being asked to consider how this new science would affect nursing education and practice.

In lectures and assignments, Elsie was asked to consider all kinds of issues relating to nursing: "What is the function of the nurse?"; "Salaries and living conditions"; "Working hours"; "Have the nursing schools met the needs of nurses or of the community?" In a well-researched essay, she considered the sociological issues of French Canada, and concluded, idealistically:

"The problem of Canada seems to be that the basis of understanding must be broadened on a realistic rather than a diplomatic basis;that is, with mutual respect, for each group has something to give the other, and something to learn from the other. The French and English may never be wholly one, but they can learn to understand one another, as all must try to do throughout the world, if future wars are to be averted."[8]

Lofty ideals were treated with respect here, even put into practice. In her notes, Elsie quotes such visionaries as Sir George Newman, onetime Medical Officer of Health for England:

"We stand today at the door of opportunity and upon us of this generation has been imposed the duty of laying the foundations of a new epoch. It is true that better and wiser men have gone before us and we enter into their labours as better men will follow us and enter into ours. But our responsibility is none the less sure. Knowledge, clearness of mind, the broad vision, strength of will and sympathy of heart have been in the past and will be in the future, the inspiration of all high endeavour."

Sir Fred Clarke, Professor of Education at McGill University, had words of inspiration too:

"Nursing most of all requires rich and liberal education as it should be the broadest and most liberal of professions.

Nursing calls for a personality peculiarly rich in inner resources and the means of preserving balance and sanity. It calls for just these refined and human traits which it is the business of a liberal education to provide."[9]

If Elsie had come here to have her faith in human nature restored after the nightmare of the war, she must have been well satisfied. In among her lecture notes, Elsie scribbled the words of Canon Barnett of Westminster Abbey: "*Fear not to sow because of the birds.*" Disraeli's words, too, appear: "The health of the people is really the foundation upon which all their happiness and all their powers as a state depend." Perhaps sensing that many of the wonderful, idealistic notions which she was embracing in Canada might be treated with scepticism in Britain, she was arming herself with these pearls of wisdom for the opposition ahead.

The British Parliament was, however, at that time considering one of the most ambitious pieces of welfare legislation ever placed before the parliament of any democratic country. In February, 1943, the government had accepted the principle of a comprehensive health service, independent of social insurance, as proposed by Sir William Beveridge, in his scheme for a welfare state where the five giants of Want, Disease, Ignorance, Squalor and Idleness would be fought.[10] Articles on the Beveridge Plan are among Elsie's papers from her year in Toronto, with notes in her own hand recording details of projected costs. A whole new sphere for working out her ideals was opening up in Britain.

A selection from the questions on examination papers for the end of the session, 1946-47, provides a flavour of how much Elsie's intellect had been stretched and stimulated during that year.

"Outline briefly and in your own words five principles of effective social relations as they apply to the 'supervisor-supervised' relationship."

"'The primary reason for the existence of universities is not to be found either in the mere knowledge conveyed to the students or in the mere opportunities for research.' [Whitehead]

a) Give the author's opinion of what a university is, and also what he considers the primary function.

b) Note the author's argument as he applies his thought to the reason for, and the conduct of, a business school in the university. You are asked to apply the author's thought just as clearly, and with detail, to any reason for the existence of a nursing school in the university."

"Discuss the educational values of night duty for student nurses. What conditions are necessary if these values are to be realised?"

On one of her essays, the lecturer commented. "Your reading is extensive. You seem to have caught the spirit of the teaching given very well."

Elsie was awarded the Certificate in Public Health Nursing (Advanced Course) in June, 1947. She and Eileen said goodbye to the many friends they had made at Toronto, and crossed the border into the United States where, through the American Nurses Association, they had arranged to spend six weeks observing nursing services in Boston, Massachusetts, New York, and Cleveland, Ohio.

In each of the cities, an intensive programme had been arranged to allow them to observe the work of the hospitals, and sightseeing had to be left for the evenings. On the way to Cleveland, they stopped over in Washington. They quickly became familiar with the Greyhound buses as the cheapest form of travel, allowing them to sit up overnight and so avoid the cost of accommodation. The routine was that Elsie would slip on first and bag the seat beside the driver, so that they could ask him all about the country, while Eileen was left to manoeuvre the luggage on board.

After their three two-week visits in the States, they clung to their determination to see the Rockies, and so travelled to Chicago, and then Winnipeg by Greyhound bus. They stopped and worked, first in Winnipeg and then in Calgary, to make some money to continue the journey. With repleted resources they hitchhiked to the foothills of the Rockies where they walked, and camped in huts, intended to accommodate lumber men, and made fir cone fires for cooking. Banff proved too expensive for them, and finally they hitchhiked to Vancouver, where a distant relative of Eileen's provided them with a very welcome bath and a bed. Having come this far, it seemed unthinkable not to visit Victoria Island, and so they sat up on the overnight boat. When darkness fell, they lay down on deck, and some other passengers brought them blankets for warmth.

Throughout their travels, they walked into any Red Cross station they came across, made themselves known, and sometimes worked for a few days to replenish their purses. Living on a shoestring, they became enviably slim. Back in New York to catch the Queen Mary, now restored to her former glory, they found that only one berth had been booked for them. They refused to accept this piece of mismanagement, until finally a double first class cabin was found for them, and there they installed themselves, complete with their dilapidated travelling attire and ten shillings - all the money they had left. Elsie explained their position to the Chief Steward and offered him the ten shillings with the promise that brother George would be meeting them at Southampton with funds. After some initial doubts, the Steward was won over, and joined in the laughter at their plight. Eileen later commented that Elsie was one of the most determined people she had ever met.[11]

Apart from the profound ways in which this year expanded and validated Elsie's thoughts on nursing, important international links had been made. Elsie maintained her interest in the Florence Nightingale International Foundation, and later became its President. This year in Toronto had prepared her in many ways for her move into the future of British nursing.

Chapter 8

Opening Windows

Fear Not to Sow

Bill Gardner's notes claim that, on her return from Canada, Elsie was appointed Deputy Chief Matron of the British Red Cross Society. However, this claim cannot be substantiated by B.R.C.S. records, many of which were destroyed after the war. Whatever her exact status, she now embarked on various advisory missions on behalf of the Red Cross. In this capacity she travelled first to Hesse in the American Zone in Germany, to advise on nursing and welfare services, then to Singapore, North Borneo, Brunei and Sarawak, to re-establish Red Cross posts there. In 1948, she took part in the Red Cross Conference in Stockholm. Her role on these assignments was a mixture of public relations officer, confidence booster, teacher, supplies officer and visiting celebrity.

From Hesse, where she arrived on 7th November, 1947, to stay as guest of the Prince and Princess von Hessen in their beautiful home at Schloss Wolfsgarten, she visited hospitals, camps, first aid posts, children's homes and motherhouses in Darmstadt, Frankfurt and Marburg, Stuttgart, Heidelberg and Munich. Conditions she met on her visits during her three week stay showed her how much welfare workers were struggling against the odds. In Darmstadt, for instance, she visited the Elinora Heim, which had been bombed and was now under repair. Children evacuated from the hospital were housed in overcrowded accommodation, sleeping on beds adapted from air raid shelter bunks, short of clothes, nappies and mackintoshes, and mostly suffering from enteritis, malnutrition and tuberculosis.

"10th November, 1947: *Left Wolfsgarten...by horse and trap for Egelsbach Station. People on train looked cold, hungry, a few eating dry bread, a real sense of dejection, many youths sleeping, no real show of friendliness or interest in my uniform."*[1]

Her visits ranged from first aid posts and rest rooms in Frankfurt's railway station, to a 12th century castle, part of which had been converted into a hospital, to a 700 bedded military hospital, filled to overflowing with patients from Russian prisoner of war camps, suffering from malnutrition, hunger, oedema and tuberculosis. She described the residents of a camp for ex-prisoners from Russia:

"Men are happy to be back, very satisfied with camp conditions, all appeared gaunt, heads shaven, some very poor, clothing in varying conditions, eyes a haunted yet expectant look. Appeared very hungry, were ravenously attacking food."[2]

The visits continued, the lists of shortages grew: insulin, glucose, drugs, nappies, stockings and shoes for nurses.

The morale of German Red Cross nursing staff was at a low ebb, after the impact of the Nazi movement. The Third Reich had put male Nazis in positions of authority in the Red Cross, dissolved the association of motherhouses, and subordinated the sisterhoods to the presidency of the Nazi-held Red Cross.3 Often Elsie found herself addressing pale, overworked nurses, who had to sleep in small rooms off the ward, with little opportunity for recreation from their work. She would remind them of Germany's historical contribution to the growth of the nursing profession, of the work of Pastor Fliedner and the Deaconesses at Kaiserwerth, from whom Florence Nightingale had drawn much of her inspiration. Nurses in Germany should be proud of their heritage, she told them:

"Today in every country there is a shortage of nurses. You are not alone by far, and nurses as a body must go forward to remedy this, as there is no other profession that offers such a deep satisfaction to women as nursing. Varying forms of training are being tried out in America, Canada, and some of the Scandinavian countries, and we at home are also contemplating radical changes."[4]

She described the problems besetting the nursing profession in many countries: the professional insularity, due in part to the long hours, the exacting work, the lack of opportunity to mix with other professions or even to enjoy a social life outside the hospital. She suggested self-help remedies for these ills. They should invite members of other professions to come and speak to them about their work, they should organise study sessions among themselves, they should visit places of interest, start art or language classes, find out about nursing in other countries. She was metaphorically opening windows, letting in a breath of cold fresh air, plumping up cushions to boost morale.

"I realise how difficult things are for you just now, yet we all in each country have difficulties and each of you can do so much to help yourselves, and others. When the time comes that we can once again visit each others' countries freely you will be so glad that you have broadened your knowledge, for daily we can learn, and I am sure you will agree that in nursing we never cease learning."[5]

Letters of appreciation followed Elsie back to Britain. Oberin Tobroth of Marburg thanked her

"for the kind and friendly way in which you expressed your appreciation of us and our point of view. I hope you have already heard how much you raised the spirits of the sisters. We were especially grateful for the universal moral support given to our work, which is an active principle of the Red Cross. We have also to thank you for the friendly statement concerning the inclusion of the German Sisters in the world-wide circle of all Sisters, and helping them to take part in the general work."[6]

Margaret von Hessen wrote to Elsie telling her how one little boy was so much in love with her that he prayed every night for her to come back.

Even on the journey to Singapore, her next port of call, Elsie, in her Red Cross uniform, found herself called upon to help other passengers. She was asked to look after a very deaf and nervous old lady, who had never left home before, and then to have a word with another passenger with two young children:

"Could not manage lunch but did not disgrace myself. The captain asked me to visit another lonely passenger with two small children and reassure her - the Red Cross was needing reassuring, but dosed them all with barley sugar and heard where they were going, etc. This helped us all."[7]

Far from finding these responsibilities onerous, Elsie grew fond of her elderly charge, who proved a source of fun throughout the journey:

"She really is a dear soul. The latest is that she thinks she had better sleep in all her clothes - advised strongly against this so, left at her door she said, 'Well I think I'd better keep my corsets on in case I forget them.' This was too much for me!"

Stops in Augusta, Basra, Bahrain and Karachi allowed for refreshment and more mirth, as Elsie's patient walked in the night and returned to the wrong room. On 22nd March, they landed on the Ganges and had breakfast on a houseboat. Rangoon affected Elsie with its poverty and bomb damage, the rickets and skin infections evident amongst the children.

"In the cool of the evening a few of us walked to the small Pagoda, frequent looks of admiration at the small children with us, and salutes to my uniform. Followed by numerous rickshaw

boys wanting us to take a ride...What a lot of help these people need."

She was clearly filled with compassion for the suffering she saw around her at this period, as well as convinced that the Red Cross could improve conditions. And so, when she met a certain amount of ill will towards the Red Cross in Singapore - there were those who felt that the Red Cross and all the other relief organisations had been strangely silent during Singapore's hour of need - she saw this as simply another problem to solve.[8]

Over dinner in Government House, on arriving in Singapore, she discussed general welfare conditions with members of the welfare organisations and government officials. Once more her time was devoted to fact-finding and morale-boosting. She visited feeding centres where children received a free meal, a drink of milk or cocoa and lessons in using the spoon, talked to moral welfare workers, and met concerned individuals to whom she could promote the work of the British Red Cross Society. Having seen the shortages, Elsie began to organise supplies, using her powers of persuasion on an official of the Straights Steamship Company, who promised to make deliveries to North Borneo free of charge.

She left Singapore in no doubt that the Red Cross could contribute significantly to the teaching of health and welfare and the stimulation of a sense of service among the people there. She proposed a peace-time programme, stressing the world-wide connections of the Red Cross and aimed particularly at the younger generation, the physically handicapped and welfare work.

At the end of the war in 1945, North Borneo had been a land of sickness, starvation and dejection. In the crowded internment camps, packed with men, women and children, people were dying on the bare floors of the huts. Towns and villages had been gutted. Jesselton and Sandakan, the two main centres, had been reduced to mounds of rubble. Of 890 government buildings, 614 were totally destroyed and 266 damaged.[9]

By the time Elsie arrived in March, 1948, a temporary order had been restored, although there were still immense difficulties, mainly in the form of shortages, ill health, lack of transport and poor sanitation. Her brief was to survey the needs of the country, to start a Red Cross branch, and to provide whatever welfare teaching was possible.

From her very first day there she noted how the country's material needs were inextricably bound up with its educational needs. Many of the children she saw at the child welfare centre, the hospital and the homes she visited, were suffering from skin complaints caused by vitamin deficiencies, and yet the market was well stocked with fresh fruit and vegetables. Dried milk was in short supply, and yet breast feeding was unpopular and weaning poorly handled, the main food being polished rice with no vegetable or vitamin additives.[10]

The fact-finding aspect of her mission led her into some strange, exotic and primitive situations, all of which she recorded in her diary in her customary factual style. Visiting the Leper Colony on Balhala Island, for instance, she found the 49 lepers, some chickens, ducks and two goats living in a group of huts with rubbish piled up all around. A three-day-old baby, delivered with the aid of a leper woman, could not be left on the island, and so Elsie and the doctor brought it back to the hospital, from where it would eventually be adopted.

The hospital in Jesselton had been completely burned down, and any equipment available had been left by the army. The present buildings consisted of palm leaf huts, and patients paid at different rates for the day. First and second class wards had hospital beds, sheets and other linen. Third class wards had boards and mats on the floor. Of the 59 patients in the mental hospital, 12 or more were in cages, and there was no treatment available for the others.

Infant Welfare Clinics were generally chaotic, with little accommodation, and patients requiring treatment for a variety of ailments from malaria to worms to malnutrition. Elsie vaccinated 74 children at one session, and was horrified by the deep sloughs left by previous vaccinations on the children's skin.

She visited a rubber estate, and a timber camp kampong, leaving at 7 a.m. for a two-hour journey by launch, followed by a sail through mangrove swamps in a small sampan. Sapangar Island's population was entirely made up of women and children, since all the men had been killed by the Japanese. A 16 year old boy was the headman.

Again and again she returned to the theme of lack of health education adding to the already existing problems:

Saturday, May 1st, 1948 (Papar): *Went in and out of several homes, the kampong type very poor. In each home two or three cases of malnutrition seen, so much of this is due to complete lack of understanding. No idea of infant feeding. Some type of daily distribution of milk would be a great assistance both to the malnourished and as a teaching scheme...*

Sunday, May 2nd, 1948: *Up early to see the weekly market, when people came in from the island areas, some beautiful sarongs and native hats. A fair amount of native fruits, fish, some meat and vegetables. Appeared to be a real meeting place, where your few things were sold and then you retired to the Chinese shop for jewels, gold and silver coins made into belts, earrings, etc...or the coffee shop. Followed some of the people with children. All the money was being spent on ornamentation, no buying of staple food, except rice.*

After more than a month of such visits she admitted to feeling very stiff (perhaps due to some of the unorthodox modes of transport) and more than ready for a break. Instead of that she was en route for Brunei on 5th May. Here she found the hospital well run, with a trained nurse in charge. "What a difference it makes to a place." was her diary comment. Supplies and drugs were adequate. This was a rich state.

In areas of deprivation, Elsie had found people interested and receptive to the idea of Red Cross work. Here among the rich in Brunei she found suspicion and rejection. Many of the people she met felt they were well enough cared for, and showed a bland indifference to "good work." One trained nurse felt that the Red Cross V.A.D.s had done a poor job in India, and therefore she did not wish to become involved with Red Cross activities. Another group of Europeans had done some sewing for the Red Cross before and during the war, and had not been thanked for their work. Elsie listened, "ate various types of Indian food and made the peace." Her diary notes understandably lacked their usual verve.

This would be a good area for a Branch. In time it would come, but we would need someone out for a period to get things really going - a real experience of true commercially minded people with little real human feeling. There is a real need for Red Cross work among the women as they have a good deal of leisure time...Tact plus plus is needed in this place.

In Sarawak, one visit took her on a three-quarter hour tramp through the jungle to a kampong, where she was the first white woman ever to have visited.

"A jungle track, bamboo poles only to cross streams and mud areas, we were guided by two Dayaks who we picked up on the road. Met a little way from the village by one of the Chief Men - a real pirate, all very friendly. Everyone out to meet us, much handshaking, and all the women surrounded me and tried to

show me their home first. All the people wore was a short sarong, brass and metal belts, some brass rings round their legs and arms, earrings. Most of the children were in the nude, the young women covered their breasts, but apparently after marriage they uncovered them. Children up to three or four were suckling at the breast, a good deal of malnutrition.

The village consisted of one long house with twenty doors and then another opposite with twelve doors, the headman had a house at the end for himself and his relatives. Rice the main diet, little signs of any other food, a few roots, paddy collected only a few weeks so they were well off...Pigs and chickens living under the long house and clearing away all the excreta, etc. - no latrines - all excreta passes through the floor to the pigs. A friendly, polite people, an alive interest, education and health teaching alongside would mean a great deal. Yaws, conjunctivitis, ? T.B., seemed to be chief troubles - the Headman not at all worried as to conditions or to health of his people. It had been a good paddy year, so all was well.

Itching to get to work among these people, so sadly said goodbye - we should really try and help them."

In another kampong, she found herself delivering a baby:

"So into one of the rooms, accompanied by the D.O., and the village, we went. Sitting between three decrepit women, an old man and the husband was the patient, completely nude, the whole of the abdominal area covered in beetle [sic] nut.

Asked if they had soap and water, turned out the relatives except the old cronies and left the wise woman who I discovered in one corner of the hut. A baby was delivered, after hastening things up, and after insisting on the safe delivery of afterbirth and washing of the baby I left, knowing all the old treatments would be carried out. (Am sorry the Red Cross to these people will mean someone to deliver babies.)"

Royalty figured among her encounters too.

Visited a model kampong area and the uncrowned king of Borneo - he has 16 children, found his youngest infant ill with enteritis. After a lot of persuasion wife agreed to come into the hospital with the child. Told him of Red Cross and its work. He said they wanted a place for their children as so many died. Asked if any of the girls about 16 to 18 years would be ready to learn. He said they could find two now.

Elsie's genius for winning people's confidence provoked some heart-rending situations. A woman she met in Sandakan asked her if she could make inquiries about having her eight year old son brought out from England where he was staying with his uncle. A nurse burst into tears when Elsie asked her about her patients: they had nothing for babies to wear in the hospital. Elsie bought ten yards of material to make clothes for them. There were signs now and then that her visits were giving encouragement to the people she met.

The joy of Miss Bates in unpacking the few things I had taken up was unbelievable. She said it was the first time she had received any help with her work...Miss Bates is the only European nurse working outside among the people.

Following her brief to set up Red Cross posts, she found some resistance in Labuan, but gradually felt that people were beginning to warm to her towards the end of her visit. No opportunity was missed. On the plane from Labuan to Kuching she met an oil director whom she had already met in Serai, and persuaded him to make moves towards setting up a Red Cross there.

In Kuching, she visited schools, talked to the Red Cross branch, attended cocktail parties where she made contacts, agreed on actions, and found recruits. One recurring subject of discussion was the need for a medical launch, what design would be most suitable and how much it would cost. She made no promises but felt "it is certainly something that would have untold value." In Sibu, she made an impression on the D.O. and Commissioner of Police. "They were both anti-Red Cross on receipt of telegram, after tea ready to cooperate," read her diary for the day.

Somehow she managed to find time for teaching, too. In Sandakan, she delivered lectures on home nursing and tropical medicine, arranged for doctors and nurses to carry on the work with a first aid course, and for the Red Cross to send out first aid and home nursing manuals. The tropical hygiene course she felt to be unsuitable for here. If a suitable course could not be found "we must get down to one ourselves", she reported.

She demonstrated baby bathing at the infant welfare clinics, was involved in discussions about school buildings, haggled over the price of para cloth for Red Cross sewing groups, spoke to natives who had just walked for four days through the jungle carrying their goods to sell at the market, arranged stores for Red Cross branch equipment, negotiated for Red Cross goods to be imported free of customs duty, and did the shopping for cots, material, castor oil and Epsom salts.

Sometimes she was so shocked by the conditions she found that she could not see how to start health education:

Any teaching value is lost, as the most elementary standards are not available - no latrines, no water...

Visited the school - a very poor collection, ragged, unclean, no latrines, no water, mud floors - standard very poor...

For all that, the need for education came across again and again:

Four men said, at different times, that their women wanted to know how to care for their children, but there was no one to teach them - even now very few girls are in school.

Now and then she had to soothe ruffled feelings before she had any cooperation: one group of Malay, Chinese, Eurasian and European women displayed "a fair amount of pettiness and difficulties even to tears. Necessary to give a good deal of time to one or two rather neurotic women but cleared up most of their troubles." But she remained patient and understanding, noting that a great deal of guidance would be needed for the Malay women who "have taken very little part in activities outside the home."

From the very basics of life, Elsie was able to swing to the highest ideals, and to continue to see her practical skills as a nurse in the light of ultimate human values. Her unique presence as a speaker endowed the words she spoke to groups in schools, hospitals and community halls with a solemnity which could cross barriers.

It is the spirit of giving and not of taking we want to teach, love and care for all people...'Loving kindness to one's fellow men in the battle field of life'.

For all her ceaseless activity, she did have the occasional moment to enjoy the countryside, rich with paddy fields, jungle, kingfishers and purple orchids and the occasional crocodile. But even Elsie's considerable resources of energy began to flag during this posting. She confided in a letter home that a secretary would have helped as "I am about to the stage of thinking Red Cross night and day."[11] A septic finger began to trouble her, and she had to have it lanced, without anaesthetic. Later penicillin was prescribed and once more the finger was lanced. "Thank goodness for Dr. Lesoeur's stiff brandy", she commented. In spite of this, she continued with her round of talks, visits and arrangements. Instead of her scheduled day of rest on returning to Singapore, she had tea with the High Commissioner, Malcolm McDonald, and he promised more help for the Red Cross. When she finally reached London at midnight on Wednesday, June 8th, she had not had a day off since March 18th.

In an article she later wrote for the Red Cross Quarterly Review, Elsie described the Dyak as "a friendly and sturdy little people, living in a very primitive way, and very keenly interested to hear of the Red Cross activities, aims and ideals". Despite her somewhat patronising description of "loyal, brave little people", her respect for the people she had met shines through. She did not deny the natives of Borneo their right to believe that the spirits of the dead went to Kinabolu. She merely wanted them to see the undeniable good sense of healthy ways of living.

"Dusans, Muruts and Bajaus were some of the head-hunting tribes in times past; they are brave and friendly people...Many of them are primitive in their habits, and it is here that the Red Cross can help by assisting with the spread of preventive health teaching, good dietary knowledge and simple child care, Nursing and First Aid talks."[12]

Her official report on the posting paid tribute to the government for the restoration work carried out since the Japanese occupation. She had collected and recorded a miscellany of facts on the history, geographical features, population and racial distribution, transport, products and customs of the country. Her report makes concise recommendations, with costs.

Although the medical launch she recommended was not immediately available, her dream was to come true in 1975, eight years after her death. A launch named "The Elsie Stephenson" was blessed on November 15th, 1975, at Kuching, by the Reverend Harry Tennant.[13]

Elsie was one of the seven British Red Cross members who attended the XVIIth International Red Cross Conference, held from August 20th to August 30th, 1948, in Stockholm. British government observers were also present, concerned with the revision of the Geneva Conventions and the proposals for the future protection of citizens in time of war.[14] Sweden gave the Conference a royal welcome, in the persons of their King, Crown Prince and Princess. Fifty-six nations were represented, most by their governments as well as their Red Cross Societies. Meetings took place in the Parliament House of Sweden, each group behind its national flag. National and political barriers were broken down, as Jews and Arabs, Greeks and Turks, Americans and Japanese, Hindus and Moslems, held constructive and peaceful discussions.

Dame Emily Blair and Elsie Stephenson, attending the Health, Nursing and Social Services Commission, were involved in discussions on such divergent subjects as the International Red Cross's continued involvement with the Florence Nightingale International Foundation, a subject obviously near to Elsie's heart, and the training of nursing auxiliaries, of great significance since the Red Cross V.A.D.s had played such a vital part in the nursing contribution to both World Wars. Here among the policy makers, Elsie had unmistakably bridged the gap between "doer" and "thinker."

The Conference ended by recalling that all sides in World War II had respected the ban on the use of poison gases and bacteriological warfare, and by urging nations to abandon the atomic bomb, the use of which would imperil civilisation itself.

In Lord Woolton's Conference Report to the Sunday Times, he described the delegates as "an impressive gathering of great personalities...men and women worthy to stand on a world stage, people of vast experience." The Conference had proved, he felt, that the people of the world regarded the preservation of the Red Cross as a matter of international importance.

Among the government observers at this conference was Bill Gardner of the War Office. He and Elsie met briefly as they checked in at the purser's office on the steamer from

Tilbury to Gothenburg, and the next day found themselves teamed up together for a deck game which they won, as Bill claimed years later, thanks to Elsie's concentration and quiet efficiency. On the train from Gothenburg to Stockholm, Bill noticed Elsie again, as she not only held her own, but steadfastly demolished the arguments of his companion, a General, in a discussion about nurses. As Bill recalled, "presently he left the field and I was left sitting opposite this 'little' [in stature] nurse and beginning to be aware that here was someone out of the ordinary."

On the Sunday morning Bill and Elsie were the only two delegates to attend the English church service. Their friendship was founded during these days in Stockholm, although Bill was at the time a happily married man (later, a widower). He recognised in the following years that the basis of a great love and understanding was laid during his long discussions with Elsie in Stockholm about "the meaning and purpose of life."

For Elsie, the conference reinforced her commitment to the ideals of the Red Cross. "We have lived through great days," she said in a talk about the Red Cross, "taken part in great events, and stood in the light of a great experience...We must pass on that experience, maintain that great comradeship and still pursue our great cause."[15]

Chapter 9

A Better Future at Home

Fear Not to Sow

July 5th, 1946, was the appointed day for the implementation of the National Health Service Act in Britain. Elsie had been impressed with the Beveridge Report, the philosophical paper on which the National Health Service (NHS) was based, when she was in Canada. With her wealth of Red Cross experience behind her, now was the ideal moment for her return to Britain where she might expect to be able to use her talents and see her hopes become reality.

It was to Suffolk she returned, where the familiarity of her surroundings allowed her to put into perspective the effects of war on people. In her Red Cross work, although she had seen the devastation, she had not been able to compare the situation before and after. Now she was at home, and, like her hospital patients returning home after an illness, she was forced to assess how much things had changed, how the health services would have to adapt, and what was the way forward.

Dr. Rogers recalled the occasion:

"I had...taken on the County Medical Officer's job in East Suffolk. Then came the new Health Service and I needed a Chief Nursing Officer to be in charge of the Health Visiting and District Nursing Services. I got her [Elsie] to come down to Ipswich for an interview. I remember how trim she looked, still in her Red Cross uniform. The Chairman of the Public Health Committee, Mrs. Fison, now Lady Fison, was with me at the interview. She was very impressed and the result was that once again Elsie Stephenson was on the Staff but on

91

a higher plane. She worked very hard reorganising the service, and it was a hard row. She was an idealist."[1]

Her task, like that of everyone implementing the new scheme, was immense. Shortage of nurses had always been an acute problem, and after the war the shortage was even greater. Recruitment was hampered by the reduction in the number of single women in the population. Gradually, male nurses, part-timers and married women were playing a greater role, and the old order of spinsters totally dedicated to nursing was fading into the past.[2] Continuity of care was therefore more difficult to achieve. Elsie was prepared to see the positive side of these changes, in the sense that nurses would now have a broader outlook, and patients would be treated more as human beings, and less as helpless dependants.

Realising the sensitive nature of her position, Elsie wrote to her nursing colleagues at Christmas, 1948, promising to meet them in the New Year. Referring to her predecessor in the job, she wrote:

"You must all be feeling the loss of such a dear friend and be very apprehensive about the future.

I can assure you that my one wish is that the future will bring us closer together so that we may all work as a progressive and happy family for the benefit of the community and for the nursing profession as a whole...

If you are in Ipswich do not hesitate to come in to County Hall as you will always be welcome."

East Suffolk County Council covered an area of 546,607 acres, and served a population of 215,812, when Elsie took over as County Nursing Officer. Her staff consisted of a Deputy County Nursing Officer, 19 health Visitors, 7 midwives, 60 district nurse midwives, and 6 general nurses. The high number of district midwives was vital in 1949 when

2,327 babies were delivered at home in East Suffolk. Elsie's plans included the increase of the health visitor and midwifery staff.[3]

The Medical Officer of Health allowed her a great deal of freedom to develop the public health, district nursing and home help services, as well as the infant welfare centres and the health education programme throughout the county. Supplies and equipment were her first concern, and she aimed to correct shortages of screens, washing facilities, towels, teaching aids, scales, fire guards, maps, files, bags and cases for health visitors. Before sweeping clean, it is wise to purchase a new broom!

Her next concern was about staff education. No arrangements seemed to stand for staff to attend the office in order to keep in touch with administrative staff, and no plans existed for in-service education. By March, 1949, she was contacting Miss Olive Baggally of the Florence Nightingale International Foundation to ask her assistance in setting up a study weekend for health visitors:

"They have done very little in the way of teaching, either in the Centres or Schools, and the need for such teaching is very great...The plan I have in mind is for lectures on the principles of teaching to take place on the Friday morning, a discussion group and your lecture on the Friday afternoon; on the Saturday morning a further lecture on the principles of teaching and in the afternoon a formal discussion group again. This would give the Health Visitors some idea of the value of teaching and the preparation of talks, and perhaps could be the beginning of further study weekends."[4]

She soon had collected details on each area covered by East Suffolk County Council: the number of districts per area, the parishes, the populations, the number of cases - midwifery, maternity and general - attended by her staff, the health visitor case load, the age and qualifications of her district nurses, their length of service, past, and expected for the future, any postgraduate courses taken, whether or not they had the certificate for administration of gas and air, and the adequacy of their housing for the storage of nursing equipment and for transport.

According to form, Elsie remained interested in the teaching of good health habits to school children. She herself undertook lectures on personal hygiene to girls, as part of a scheme of lectures for schools designed to make the children appreciate: "the importance of health to the individual and the family; the wonder of the body, with a talk on simple anatomy and physiology; the dangers of neglect; the importance of a healthy mind; the importance of home and diet; the wonder of growing up and embarking on a new life; preparation for parenthood and its responsibilities."

During the sixteen months of her stay as County Nursing Officer in East Suffolk, Elsie's Deputy was Margaret Vaughan Jones, whom she had first met at Queen Charlotte's Hospital during her midwifery training. In a letter to Bill Gardner after Elsie's death, Miss Vaughan Jones recalled Elsie's work in East Suffolk:

"She coped with re-organising districts and taking over control from local Nursing Associations to the Local Authority. No easy task. She coped admirably, organising meetings throughout the county. She would work till the early hours of the morning re-organising areas for nursing personnel...The welfare of the nursing staff was one of her main concerns."[5]

Flora Sandes, her old acquaintance from Yugoslavia occasionally accompanied Elsie on her rounds during this period.[6] After the war, Flora Sandes had returned from Yugoslavia to Woodbridge, where she was often to be seen travelling round the lanes in Suffolk on her motorised wheelchair.[7] What inspiration she gave to Elsie is matter for conjecture. It seems significant that Elsie made a special effort to seek her out. A common love of Yugoslavia no doubt united them, but perhaps also a recognition of the indomitable spirit and determination that they both shared.

By the time Elsie became Nursing Officer for Newcastle in 1950, she was coming to terms with the new Health Service and discovering how to make it work for her. With responsibility for coordinating the work of health visitors, district nurses, midwives, nursery nurses and home helps, as well as for the local authority training schemes for all these services, she was in a powerful position to put her policies into practice.

Fortunately, she arrived in Newcastle at a "remarkable period in health and welfare service in Newcastle-upon-Tyne."[8] Miss Dorothy Ross Gibson who was Matron of Newcastle General Hospital, provided a warm welcome for Elsie's idea of creating links between hospital and community. At the same time Sir James Spence, Nuffield Professor of Child Health was cooperating with Newcastle's Chief Medical Officer to improve the maternal and child welfare services in the area. Elsie was inevitably drawn into this atmosphere of enthusiasm.

Looking at the picture presented to her when she arrived in Newcastle, in an effort to assess the effects of the N.H.S. after one year's operation, she concluded that the responsibility of the public health sector in the domiciliary service had increased considerably since the inception of the Health Service. The real problems, as she saw them, were "social and human, the direct result of our way of life."The cost of living was rising, she felt, driving more women to work, and leaving no one at home to attend to the children and the old people. "The problem of the care of the elderly is a very real one," she noted prophetically.

Many of the services which would later be seen as hospital problems were at that stage being dealt with in the community. Premature babies, for instance, were often nursed in their own homes

"under conditions which seemed, at first sight, quite unsatisfactory, if not impossible. Experience has proved that the really important things are the personality of the premature baby nurse and her ability to mobilise the services of all the members of the family - sometimes friends and neighbours - and to organise them into a keen enthusiastic team working for the baby's welfare."[9]

Simultaneously, the number of hospital confinements was rising, due in part to the fact that maternity services were now free of charge, and that poor housing conditions made home confinements less attractive. For midwives, this meant that they were less likely to attend deliveries themselves, and more likely to assist the doctor in the role of maternity nurse and then to visit the new mother at home after delivery. As a result, it was difficult to find enough home confinements to provide student midwives with the necessary experience to complete their training. Besides this, midwives were now being used to accompany patients to hospitals and nursing homes in the city and to outside hospitals, all of which put an added strain on the midwifery service.

Elsie's annual report further claimed that the health visitor's field of action had greatly increased under the N.H.S. to include the whole family, and not simply mother and baby. "It is hoped that the cooperation between General Practitioners (G.P.s) and Health Visitors will increase, and that the G.P.s will realise how much Health Visitors may assist in the health education of the families which they attend." She also reported an increase in demand for the home nursing service, which was running smoothly. Mutual benefits were apparent for home nurses and hospital nurses from the increased cooperation between the two groups, she claimed.

Thanks to the climate of cooperation in Newcastle at that time and to the 1949 Nurses' Act authorising the General Nursing Council to approve experimental training schemes, she was able to introduce a scheme allowing student nurses in general training to spend some time with nurses in the community. Newcastle General Hospital was the first to participate in 1951, and later students from the Royal Victoria Infirmary, Fleming Memorial Children's Hospital and Walkergate Infectious Diseases Hospital were included.[10] Now, at last, Elsie was in a position to help student nurses see the concept of nursing she had admired at Toronto University, where "the hospital to which our patients come and where we train our nurses has to be seen, not as an end in itself, but as merely one episode in the individual's life-long endeavour to preserve the structural and functional integrity which we call health."[11]

This cooperation between the hospital and community sides of nursing was so fundamental to Elsie's belief in the role of the nurse in society that she herself briefed the student nurses who were about to go out on community secondment.[12] Her friend, Margaret Freeman, was a dietician in the Newcastle hospitals at the time, and recalls how some of the students reacted to this insight into how the other half lived. "I remember one young student coming back absolutely shattered, and she said 'I don't think we can do much with this generation. We'll have to concentrate on the next.'"[13]

Another source suggests that Elsie's influence was strong throughout the nursing services in Newcastle. Collecting evidence from health visitors in Newcastle on why they had chosen this specialty, an independent observer made the following comment:

"Their answers hardly differed, even in phrasing. They said, while nursing, they had realised that patients in a hospital came from homes and belonged to families. They became curious about these homes and families, and realised how important a factor they were in patient's condition and recovery."[14]

There can be little doubt that Elsie's encouragement of such attitudes helped to create a united sense of purpose in the community nursing services, and to some extent in the hospital sector in Newcastle at that time. Elsie described this new approach in a paper published in 1953:

"In the majority of cases the health visitor entering the field of public health does so because she has realised the importance of social and environmental and preventive teaching in the field of curative medicine, and that mental and physical health cannot be separated... Today we have realised that the hospital is only a very small part of the real service to the community."[15]

At the same time, she was dabbling in the training for health visitors and district nurses in her area, although with perhaps less success that she enjoyed with the hospital-community liaison. Her own report on health visiting in Newcastle, 1955, hints at some of the problems.

"The recruitment of student health visitors continued to be poor, however, the standard of students applying was of a good level. The preventive service will never have the attraction of the other services, yet the health visitor of the future, no less than her sister of the past, must have a true vocation for this great work. We are as yet in the dawn of the National Health Service and the health visitor must not be afraid of joining hands with her sisters in all fields to create the service that she has so long envisaged... Recognition of this work financially could be one of the ways that promotion might be envisaged."[16]

The health visitor and district nurse training course was organised around a small family case load, supervised by a qualified health visitor. Although those who successfully completed the course received the qualification of health visitor from the Royal Society of Health, official recognition from the Royal College of Nursing was lacking. In fact, Elsie created a rather poor impression of herself in the Royal College by consulting experts there for advice on setting up courses, without admitting that she intended to go ahead and do so in Newcastle.[17]

This entrepreneurial spirit was typical of how Elsie was handling many aspects of her life now, and there is no evidence that she minded ruffling a few official feathers in the pursuit of her aims. Her convictions about the central nature of the work of the public health nurse led her to spread her own net wider. She became a member of Newcastle Women's Civic Committee where, according to the Chairman: "You have given the Committee what it so badly lacks - vitality, ideas, and an enthusiastic understanding of what it could achieve."[18]

There was talk of her becoming a Justice of the Peace, although this did not materialise. She was a strong advocate of the teaching of family planning, even to Catholic women.[19] A Catholic member of staff put up some opposition to this, but Elsie insisted that nurses were obliged to provide health education, whatever their own persuasions. She was early in the field of ante- and post-natal exercises for mothers, and she never missed the opportunity to follow up post-natal mothers.[20]

Her comment about the problem of old people had been prophetic not only in respect of the long-term effects on the National Health Service, but also in the short-term, in her own immediate family. Her mother suffered a stroke in 1950, and could no longer stay alone in Newmarket, and so Elsie had her to live with her in Newcastle. No more apt testing ground could have been found for her to put her convictions into practice. A series of home helps arrived to deal with the old woman, who was almost totally dependent and extremely demanding. One by one, they left. Salvation finally arrived in the form of Heidi, a Swiss au pair intent on improving her English. "The old lady...at first didn't like a foreign girl to look after her. (At the beginning of my stay I sometimes was glad not to understand everything she said to me!)"[21]

Heidi, along with other friends who knew Elsie in Newcastle, recalls how Mrs. Stephenson could at times be very unkind to Elsie, but only ever received patience and sympathy in return. The day Elsie first took her mother out in a wheelchair is one that Heidi will never forget. Mrs. Stephenson kept up such a volume of screaming and grumbling that the walk had to be rapidly curtailed to avoid further embarrassment.

It was in Newcastle that Elsie first had the opportunity to become involved in serious surveys connected with nursing. Sir James Spence's *1000 Families in Newcastle,* was a study of family life in the area, published by Oxford University Press in 1954, which showed up areas, such as child morbidity, where the energies of the welfare services should be concentrated. Health visitors helped collect data for this study, which Elsie supported in every way she could. "Each new generation of mothers in its turn needs practical advice and demonstration," the report stated, "and the emphasis of advice changed in social conditions and advances in knowledge."

The health visitors were also asked to cooperate with data collection for a study of chronic bronchitis in the community. In particular the information was collected concerning sex and age incidence and the social and occupational environment of chronic bronchitics compared to an equal number of controls. Newcastle University and the Royal Victoria Infirmary were involved in the study, facts which Elsie saw fit to include in her report for the year 1955.

The study which perhaps brought her the most recognition during her time in Newcastle, however, was the Jameson Report,*An Inquiry Into Health Visiting,* H.M.S.O., London, 1956. Sir Wilson Jameson chaired the working party, which consisted of the Medical Officer of Health for Oxford, a General Practitioner who was Vice-Chairman of Birmingham Executive Council, a lady Alderman who was Chairman of Bradford Health Committee, and two nurses, Miss E. Himsworth, County Nursing Officer for Midlothian and Peebles, and Elsie Stephenson.

The working party met twenty-two times in London and six times in other centres. Miss Himsworth recalls how Elsie worked tirelessly on the project, and how she endeavoured to gain recognition and status for health visitors on a committee dominated by medical men. The text of the report is so close to many of the ideas Elsie was putting into practice in Newcastle that one feels she must have exerted a considerable amount of influence on its compilation, or else she was lucky to find herself among like-minded people. Some ideas are similar to thoughts Elsie expressed in addresses on health visiting during and after her time in Newcastle. Miss Himsworth felt that Elsie had a breadth of vision and experience out of the ordinary among nurses of her day.

Essentially the Jameson Report described the role of the health visitor as that of family adviser. Anything that impeded her in carrying out that role should be considered of secondary importance, and so non-essential duties in clinics, like selling vitamins, for instance, could be carried out by untrained personnel. Health visitors should operate as practitioners in their own right, from offices in their working territory, and with all necessary equipment and clerical help to hand. By the time the Jameson Report appeared, Elsie had already established that Newcastle's health visitors should work directly from home, instead of checking in at a central office before going out on visits. This implied a conceptual change in the status of health visitors, who were now being trusted to act as responsible to their own code of professional practice.[22]

The university connections with health visitor training should be fostered, the report recommended. The educational and preventive aspects of the health visitors' work should be considered crucial to the effective working of the National Health Service.

"It is not difficult to foresee a time when, with full cooperation between the medical officer of health and the general practitioner, both curative and preventive service for the family at home will become an integral part of general practice."[23]

A paragraph in the report describing the inadequacy of nurse training to foster the kind of attitudes necessary for a good health visitor might have been written by Elsie, whose views on traditional nursing training had become clear during her year in Toronto.

"Hospital training has been institutional in character and has provided little or no opportunity for treating patients as whole persons....The long period in curative nursing has made the adjustment to a preventive outlook difficult. The necessary obedience of the student nurse to those in authority has produced an attitude difficult for some nurses to shake off when undertaking health visitor training. The unquestioned authority of nurses over their patients in hospital has made it difficult for some to refrain from adopting the same attitude in the relationship with clients at home."[24]

With such comments in mind, the report recommended that the General Nursing Council's syllabus for nurse training should include experience in people's homes. Elsie had obviously had much to say on this subject.

The Jameson Report was greeted with scepticism in some circles. The Royal College of Nursing objected to its recommendation for a new grade, somewhere between general and administrative staff, a step towards administrative and teaching posts. The College saw the skills required for administrative and for teaching as totally divergent. Elsie, however, was never one for demarcation, and here her interest would lie in what the two disciplines could learn from each other, rather than in developing their separate characteristics. A second objection was that the Jameson Report failed to define the knowledge base for health visiting. After publication, people were as uncertain as ever as to the exact nature of the health visitor's work, and therefore which subjects she should study to prepare for her job. By the mid-1960s, the *Health Visitors' and Social Work Training Act, 1962,* had become law and the general climate of opinion was that health care must look beyond the confines of the hospital walls to be effective.[25]

Elsie was being consulted as an authority on many aspects of nursing now. She was a member of the World Health Organisation Advisory Panel of the Expert Committee on Nursing, and a member of the W.H.O. Expert Committee on Midwifery. At a W.H.O. course at Vevey, Switzerland, Elsie represented the public health angle, while Dame Elizabeth Cockayne, Chief Nursing Officer at the Ministry of Health, represented nursing in general. Dame Elizabeth was immediately impressed with Elsie's enthusiasm and warmth.

"Elsie always had the light and amusing touch which enabled her to make early contact with all those attending. Her experience with the Red Cross had also helped her to bridge many gaps. I spent some time with her between sessions hoping to discover her actual work in Newcastle which gave rise to her tremendous enthusiasm."[26]

In Newcastle, Elsie had been given the opportunity to bring together many of her convictions about nursing, to try out her theories and to assess their practicability. Her 1955 Report on Health Visiting expressed her belief in the furrow she had ploughed.

"A new service awaits the families, with the Medical Officer of Health at the helm; the general practitioner as clinical leader, and the health visitor as the pivot of health, social and nursing services, with the experts assisting where necessary - the home nurse, the midwife, and the social worker, together going forward in this great work."

With characteristic single-mindedness, she was nonetheless able to leave the work she had done in Newcastle in order to take up a post offering her new challenges and opportunities to influence the future of nursing. On 26th May, 1956, the *Newcastle Journal* reported the departure of Miss Elsie Stephenson to take up post as Director of Nursing at the University of Edinburgh, "the first such appointment in the United Kingdom". More than two hundred officials, nurses and friends had gathered to present her with a gold watch on behalf of the public health staff and associated bodies, a token of their appreciation of her contribution to the health of the community.

Chapter 10

Placing the Coping Stone

Fear Not to Sow

The setting up of this pioneering unit at Edinburgh University was a triumph for forward-looking nurses in the medically-orientated atmosphere of Edinburgh, and a tribute to the cooperation of the Scottish Home and Health Department (S.H.H.D.), the General Nursing Council for Scotland, the Scottish Board of the Royal College of Nursing, the Rockefeller Foundation and the University. The concept of nursing as a subject worthy of study at university level went back as far as 1901, when Mrs. Bedford Fenwick asked:

"Lastly, will not Colleges of Nursing be connected with universities which will give a degree in nursing to those who satisfactorily pass through the prescribed curriculum, and so place the coping stone on the fair edifice of nursing education?"[1]

Mrs. Bedford Fenwick would perhaps have found it hard to believe that the "fair edifice" would be allowed to collect moss for 56 years before the coping stone was finally heaved into position in Britain.

The United States had moved much more quickly. Mary Adelaide Nutting had taken the first ever Chair of Nursing at Teacher's College, Columbia University (New York City) in 1907. It is interesting to compare her thoughts on the place of nursing in a university with those of an Edinburgh doctor speaking on the same topic as late as 1964.

Mary Adelaide Nutting: "University Schools of Nursing form the only hope for any genuine educational development in our work and these schools are in a sense still on trial. There are many doubtless honestly unable to believe that nursing has any need which the University could be called upon to satisfy. And there is also a stalwart body of opponents, mainly medical."[2]

Forty years on, addressing the Association of Scottish Matrons in October, 1964, Professor Ronald Girdwood claimed there was no great enthusiasm among clinicians for the idea of graduate nurses "and that many consider that this is a potential blow that may cause considerable harm to nursing as we know it in this country."

Yet Elsie had already seen how satisfactorily Toronto University dealt with nurse education, and there were already graduate nurses coming to Britain from North America, urging that nursing should be taught in universities here. One such was Gladys Carter, who had written in 1939:

"What is wanted above all else in the training schools is a high wind of criticism, and a bonfire for prejudices and outworn traditions...the establishment of an experimental training school is needed as much today as in 1860...affiliation to a university would be desirable."[3]

From 1953-56, Gladys Carter was attached to Edinburgh's Department of Public Health and Social Medicine as the first Boots Research Fellow in nursing, and during that time she was involved in preliminary plans for the Nursing Studies Unit.[4]

Proud of their Scottish heritage, many nurses in the Edinburgh establishment felt very wary of any influence from North America. Professor Girdwood played on this caution when he warned, in his 1964 speech to the Scottish Matrons Association, of the danger that the satisfactory product of the present nurse training system might give way to the nursing model prevalent in the United States, a situation, he claimed, which no British clinician with knowledge of the American system would welcome.

Against this background, the Scottish branch of the Royal College of Nursing (R.C.N.) had been pressing hard for more contact with the university. Miss Margaret Lamb had been running a Sister Tutor certificate course at the R.C.N., in collaboration with the University of Edinburgh and Moray House Teacher Training College, since 1946.[5] She had vehemently opposed medical opinion in Edinburgh that nursing was a purely practical craft with no academic content, arguing that entrants to nurse training in the large Scottish centres were all required to have the equivalent of university entrance.[6] Margaret Lamb had been selected by the Scottish Office to spend a year studying American nurse training courses at Chicago and Yale Universities, in preparation for the new venture in Edinburgh, and it was generally assumed that she would direct the new unit.

At Edinburgh University, however, the Nursing Teaching Unit Advisory Committee had obtained the University Court's authorisation to advertise the post of Director, and to appoint a Selection Committee to deal with applications. This Committee was to consist of the Dean of the Faculty of Medicine or his nominee, Dr. Richard Scott, Professors Pilley, Brotherston, Drever, Kennedy and Kellar, and two representatives from the Royal College of Nursing.[7]

The news, which broke at a conference in St. Andrews attended by high-ranking nurses from throughout the United Kingdom, that Elsie Stephenson had been appointed to the Director's post, was greeted with consternation and sheer disbelief. Other candidates for the post had been eminently qualified; one held a senior post at the Ministry of Health and was both a nurse and a doctor. Except for her certificate from Toronto University, Elsie had no academic qualifications. She was English, to the chagrin of

107

many well-qualified Scottish nurses. She was an administrator, appointed to a teaching unit. Her background was in public health, while student nurses spent most of their training days in hospital.

The job advertisement obviously attracted Elsie, given her passion for liberal university education for nurses, and her flair for innovation:

"The object of the Unit will be to assist in the provision of a regular supply of teachers, administrators and leaders in the nursing profession with high academic standards of attainment and all the advantages of close contact with the general life of the University throughout the period of their course of study."

In the historical framework, an inescapable logic points to Elsie as the candidate who suited the requirements of the time. It seems clear that the Selection Committee felt that nothing short of the "high wind of criticism" and "bonfire for prejudices and outworn traditions" prescribed by Gladys Carter would start the new unit off on the right footing. Candidates who were deeply entrenched in, or open to, influence from the establishment would therefore be excluded. Writing to congratulate Elsie on her appointment, Professor Alex Kennedy of the Department of Psychological Medicine, who had also known Elsie in Newcastle, said:

"We were looking for someone who would take a new look at nursing and not be too heavily influenced by the present structure and I don't think you will disappoint us. This could be made into the most important job in nursing."[8]

Elsie's criticisms of the nurse education system had been voiced through the Jameson Report, and her individualistic approach to nurse training had met with success and approval in Newcastle.

More than that, however, Elsie saw nursing as an art and science designed to help the individual retain his rightful place in society, and to teach him how to improve his contribution to, and enjoyment of, the community in which he lived. Nursing seen in this light fitted well into Edinburgh's gigantic Arts Faculty where the Social Science Research Centre, founded in 1949, was already ripening into the Social Science Faculty. Professor Drever, on the Selection Committee responsible for Elsie's appointment, was Chairman of the Social Science Research Centre.[9] Nursing would progress naturally from the Arts Faculty into the new Faculty of Social Science which was inaugurated in 1963.

The future for nursing, as Elsie saw it, was to become knowledge-based, while retaining the art of caring and the spirit of service. In order to be knowledge-based, nursing must develop research interests, and Elsie had already proved her appreciation of research through her work in Newcastle with Professor Spence. The time was ripe for such ideas. C.P. Snow was warning against the growing rift between scientific thought and the liberal arts, the *Two Cultures:*

"Two groups - comparable in intelligence, identical in race, not grossly different in social origin, earning about the same incomes, who had almost ceased to communicate at all."[10]

Although Elsie's public health leanings might at first sight appear to work against her selection for a post dealing with hospital-orientated nurse training, there were, at that time, some advantages in her background. The most obvious is that her public health experience might have saved her from total submersion in the hospital status quo. Beyond that, however, it was through public health training that some of the earliest connections between nursing and universities were forged, Southampton, Cardiff and Battersea Polytechnic being among the first universities with health visitor connections.[11]

For such an important development in the nursing world, official comment was mandatory, and many sections of the press were loud in their acclaim of Elsie's appointment to the post.

"Nurses will rejoice at this significant first appointment of a nurse as a member of the faculty of a British university, especially as the appointment as advertised was not limited to nurses...Nurses will join in congratulating Miss Stephenson on being selected to direct the first university nursing teaching unit in Great Britain set to prepare teachers and administrators at that fine seat of learning, the University of Edinburgh, following upon the pioneer educational work of the Scottish Board of the Royal College of Nursing."[12]

The Royal College of Nursing, however, thinly disguised its lack of enthusiasm at the committee's choice:

"As you will know, the College has worked in close conjunction with the University authorities in the launching of the Nursing Teaching Unit, and they feel that its establishment is a landmark in the history of the nursing profession."[13]

The Public Health Section of the R.C.N. recorded its recognition of the public health angle to the appointment:

"It is an encouraging sign of the times that a nurse with a public health background should be appointed to this post."[14]

If Elsie was concerned about her academic suitability for the post, there is little remaining evidence of it. She did apply to be admitted to the Health Visitor Tutors' Roll, but was turned down on the grounds that she had not completed three years as a full time health visitor. Toronto University willingly supplied her, on request, with references and evidence that she had studied there. Her anomalous position as a non-graduate was rectified in 1961, when the degree of Master of Arts was conferred on her, under the power given to the Senatus "to admit to a degree in any Faculty except the Faculty of Medicine, any Professor, Reader or Lecturer of the University who is not a graduate at the University."[15] Her fellow graduand was Mr. P. Ritchie Calder, C.B.E., whose appointment to the Chair of International Relations took effect from 1st October, 1961.[16] The two remained good friends.

In Toronto in 1947-48, Elsie had thought about the role of university education for nurses, and her notes from that period contain some apposite comments:

"What occupation more than nursing has allowed itself to be so routinised and thus allowed its enthusiastic young students to become dull, apathetic and subordinate? It should today have been a leader in the field of social science, instead it is fighting for recognition as a profession. To produce imagination, vision and thought, what better place than the university could be chosen for the very necessary moulding of the young student nurse in the care of mankind?"[17]

How to put into practice her aim to produce young nurses with imagination, vision and thought, was Elsie's task for the years ahead.

Difficulties were not hard to find when she first arrived in Edinburgh. Even finding accommodation presented problems. Kay Rowe, academic secretary of the Social Sciences Research centre was asked if there were rooms available for the Director and her secretary:

"Like all good administrators (!) I said that we had no rooms to spare, that any we had unused were earmarked for future developments. However, overnight I thought better of it and phoned him back the next day to say that we did have two rooms on the top floor of No. 40 that might be spared (half hoping that the prospect would be sufficiently unattractive not to be wanted). But I hadn't met Elsie Stephenson then, otherwise I might have known that three stories high wouldn't put her off."[18]

Elsie's irrepressible optimism saw her through the early days. She was seldom discouraged by practical problems. Her sights were firmly set on the horizon, and she celebrated each step along the way, making light of the pitfalls.

"She had a charismatic personality - boundless energy - the ability to deal with the unbelievers in the medical world."[19]

"She had a wonderful flair for persuading people to work with her (nursing, medical and general administrators), and for recognising the time to 'push' a point or 'waiting' for the right moment."[20]

Soon after she took up her post, she began looking for an assistant, and wrote to the Director of the Florence Nightingale International Foundation for help in her search:

"I do ultimately wish to find an assistant for the Unit, and would like, if possible, a nurse who is a graduate and could offer either psychiatric nursing or science as a background. If you hear of anyone whom you think might be suitable and who is interested in the progress of the profession, I will be ready at any time to see them."[21]

Gradually, the kind of staff she wanted began to arrive, attracted by the new departure, the scope for formulating their ideas, the chance to influence the future of this exciting project. As they joined the staff, members of the Unit immediately registered for first or higher degrees.

While advocating better education and status for nurses, however, she did not achieve higher salaries for staff in Nursing Studies, nor is there evidence that she even tried. Senior nurses entering the academic setting had often to settle for a drop in salary.[22] One possible explanation of Elsie's failure to fight for improved salaries is the precarious nature of the early funding of the Unit. The Rockefeller

Foundation had promised funding for five years, and Elsie must obviously have been concerned to keep the Unit viable beyond that time. This is certainly one area where nurses failed to carry through their own belief in their status in a university setting.

Beginning with a course for tutors was undoubtedly an intelligent move, although Elsie cannot claim credit for this. The Royal College of Nursing course for nurse tutors provided the basis for the two year tutor course which began at the Edinburgh unit in the 1956-57 session. Margaret Lamb, in spite of being overlooked for the Director's post, worked along with Elsie to help establish the new course. It was clear that, in order to produce student nurses with a broader view of their role, tutors themselves would have to be able to grasp these broader concepts. And so the first batch of tutor students, professional people, many of whom had not studied for years, found themselves studying First Ordinary Psychology plus another subject chosen from the syllabus, alongside fresher students straight from school. The entrance test for the course included a day-long assessment, with psychology and dexterity tests.

Students on the course were introduced to new teaching situations, which some of them viewed with suspicion. Seminars, for instance, were a new concept to many of them, as well as flannelgraphs, visual aids of all kinds, and role playing. Elsie had limitless scope for her love of innovation.[23] Once accustomed to student status, many of these tutor students registered for first degrees, and some later graduated with higher degrees.[24]

In 1958, a course for nursing administrators in hospital or public health was added, and once more students were asked to choose one subject from the Ordinary Syllabus. For some of these students, this experience was their first exposure to many of the concepts underpinning nursing. Never before had they considered nursing in its historical context or tried to visualise its place in world affairs. The entry of these nurses into a university setting represented the opening of doors into a world where questions could be asked and their answers sought, where they were given the means to find any knowledge they needed. Some found, in particular, that Elsie's public health bias allowed them to see for the first time the interface between community and hospital nursing.[25]

Given the strong international sense she had developed through the Red Cross and her war work, Elsie rejoiced at the World Health Organisation (W.H.O.) decision to establish in 1964 an International School of Nursing within the Nursing Studies Unit. Courses followed by International School students were closely associated with the diploma and certificate courses for tutors and administrators already established at the Unit. Even before the International School began, the Nursing Studies Unit had received students from England, France, Ghana, India, Ireland, Jamaica, Korea, Nigeria, Northern Ireland, Scotland, Sierra Leone, Switzerland, South Africa, Turkey, Wales and Yugoslavia. The aim of the School was to provide:

"...a contribution to the improvement of nursing care to the individual and the family, sick and well, through the development of nursing services and education in the European Region and elsewhere."[26]

This development provided another dimension to the opportunities opening up to students at the Unit. Not only were students mixing with undergraduates, but also with qualified nurses from other countries. Elsie made the most of the situation, inviting everyone to her house for evenings where social and cultural differences were left behind for the time being. It was not unusual to find 60 people crowded into Elsie's sitting room, all talking animatedly, Elsie having as much fun as her guests. In formal and informal ways, she was playing her part in ensuring the International School would live up to the expectations expressed in the University Gazette:

"This International School within the Nursing Studies Unit will give opportunities for exchange of ideas, for language development and for the creation of the highest standards of nursing care and service. Edinburgh has always been a well-known medical centre; it is perhaps not inappropriate to hope that it becomes an equally well-known and respected centre of nursing."[27]

Of all the Nursing Studies Unit's activities, the undergraduate course, set up in 1960, met with the most resistance on all fronts. The medical profession greeted the notion of graduate nurses with suspicion. From within the nursing profession the wariness towards the new course was no less. Matrons and tutors in the Edinburgh hospitals were asked to accommodate undergraduate student nurses in their wards and classrooms, to allow special teaching time for Unit staff, and to allow the students to leave their workplace as teaching time demanded. Sisters and staff nurses were uncertain how to treat this new species of student. Students in orthodox training sometimes mistrusted the newcomers for their apparent privileges and their ambitions.

The strain on undergraduates at the beginning was great, since they were expected to fulfil the normal obligations of their chosen university course while at the same time undergoing nurse training, fitting extra nursing tuition time into university terms, and practical experience in the wards during summer vacations. The dropout rate in the first five years of the course was over fifty per cent (26 out of 54 completed the course).[28]

Elsie's convictions about the need for university education for nurses, along with her personal warmth and her affinity with young people, helped the survivors to stay the course. At a time when youth culture was fired with idealism, Elsie was preparing her students to blow away the cobwebs of fusty institutions and create a more ideal world.

Jottings scribbled in her notebook record a summary of what she expected from the undergraduate course:

"a. To attract a better educated and more thoughtful type of girl.

b. To provide a more comprehensive type of training and produce a more effective nurse at the end.

{What are the criteria for efficiency?}

c. To provide a more satisfying experience for the candidate throughout her training and retain her interest.

d. To reduce wastage by more effective selection and by the greater retention of interest."

Explaining the course was a public relations exercise which the staff of the Unit undertook out of a sense of commitment. Even on Sundays, Miss Win Logan would visit the wards where undergraduate students were working, talking to the nurse in charge, and to the patients chosen for care studies. The students themselves, knowingly or not, became advertisements for their course, and many proved excellent students, both in their university, and in their nursing work.[29]

Elsie made a point of including the students in relevant decision-making. Fiona Smith recalls her class, attired in student nurses' uniforms, sitting with Elsie in the garden behind 19 Chalmers Street, discussing the design of the badge for graduates of the course. Elsie was keen that a lamp should be incorporated, but the students felt, if there was a lamp, there should also be a flame. This design was adopted.[30]

As the undergraduate course thus became more accepted, and as experience grew, it became necessary to formalise and define it. Win Logan became organiser for the resulting course which emerged in 1967, leading to the degree of B.Sc. (Soc. Sc.- Nursing).

Elsie's early contribution to the course included the idea that students should keep a day book and that each student should follow up a normal family throughout training. In a practical sense, she helped students financially by obtaining Red Cross bursaries, via her connections with the Red Cross Society.

While the Nursing Studies Unit, at 19 Chalmers Street, was developing into a haven for the students, she also helped fill their weekends by inviting them to walk with her on the Pentland Hills on Sundays, before going back to her house for tea. Her mother was still living with her, and so the organisation involved was not insignificant. It was her style to celebrate every step along the way, and to find any excuse to throw a party. When the Department was moved from Chalmers Street to George Square, the 1961-66 batch of students were sitting their state final examinations. At lunchtime, they raced over from the Royal Infirmary to the Adam Ferguson Building where, among packing cases, Elsie had a bottle of sherry and glasses for a celebration before they dashed back for the afternoon exam session.[31]

Whether or not students completed the course, Elsie maintained her personal interest in their progress. She helped find work for those who left the course, gave thinking space to those considering their future, organised a summer occupation for one with family problems, made contacts for those travelling abroad.[32]

As the various courses were gaining credibility, research interests continued to occupy staff. One of the Unit's earliest assets was Miss Audrey John, awarded a Ph.D. in 1960 for her thesis, "*A Study of the Psychiatric Nurse and His/Her Role in the Care of the Mentally Sick.*" Elsie was totally committed to research as the sound basis for professional status for nursing.

"We must promote, initiate and support research studies which include both basic and applied research, so that a body of communicable, repeatable and verifiable knowledge of nursing and its processes can be developed....There can be little doubt that our future as a profession depends very largely on our ability to look at ourselves objectively and scientifically as well as on our capacity for development and change."*33*

By the time the Unit was four years old, Elsie could claim to have initiated a fair amount of rudimentary research, on wide-ranging subjects, such as the recruitment of nurses, environmental aspects of nursing, and patients' attitudes to nursing care. Sometimes these studies served to indicate areas where much more rigorous research was necessary before any advance in knowledge could be claimed.[34]

Some later studies grew from here. The project on the importance of the environment on nurses' attitudes to their work, for instance, highlighted marriage and husband's work as being the main inducements to work in a given area. Whether knowingly or not, this work can be seen as a forerunner to the much wider study directed by Lisbeth Hockey in 1976, and carried out with her team of associates at the Edinburgh nursing department's Nursing Research Unit, on *Women In Nursing* (Hodder & Stoughton, London). This project investigated the unique problems of nurses as a female workforce, with all the attendant problems of home responsibilities.

By 1966, Elsie was able to provide a list of the subjects requiring research, bearing a remarkable resemblance, as Phyllis Runciman pointed out in her 1981 Elsie Stephenson Memorial Lecture, to the list in *Research for Nursing - A guide for the Enquiring Nurse.*"[35]

"The hygiene of the patient, his bodily cleanliness, his hair, his mouth, his pressure points; the management of the patient's physical environment - his bed, his locker, his day room; his potential contact with cross-infection; the arrangement of his waking and sleeping hours; the measurement of temperature, pulse and respiration; the administration of certain drugs, e.g. aperients; the keeping of records; the welcome of the patient and his farewell; the day-to-day encouragement of the patient and his relatives..."[36]

If her vision of the way ahead for nursing research was perceptive and accurate, her plans for the future also included the inauguration of a Chair of Nursing at Edinburgh University. To this end she arranged for fees for her advisory work on the magazine, *Midwife and Health Visitor* to be paid into a fund administered by the Secretary of the University.

"I am very anxious to obtain a Chair of Nursing here, and wish any moneys involved to go towards this...This is a new venture in nursing, and will include Health Visiting and Midwifery fields, and we are already involved with International Nurses. There are two main developments which a department like this has to develop, a research programme adequately financed, and a Chair of Nursing. This I am sure will do more for the image and development of nursing in all its aspects in this country than anything yet put forward."[37]

The idea of a chair of nursing goes back at least to Mrs. Bedford Fenwick and her pronouncements of 1901, and was later reinforced by the Florence Nightingale International Foundation, set up in 1934 with the aim of improving education for nursing, and the intention of instituting a chair of nursing at Bedford College, University of London.[38]

After Elsie's death, the Special (Elsie Stephenson) Nursing Studies fund was started, with the hope of funding the chair and naming it after Elsie Stephenson. It was not until

1972, however that Elsie's successor, Margaret Scott Wright, became Britain's first Professor of Nursing. Much to her widower's disappointment, the Chair was not named after Elsie. The funds collected eventually combined with her widower's to become the Gardner Bequest, which is still used by the Nursing Studies Department to help finance research projects. Elsie's visionary qualities and her dynamism continue to be recognised by the Nursing Studies Department, where the *Elsie Stephenson Memorial Lecture* regularly acknowledges her contribution to the progress of the nursing profession.

Chapter 11

Raising the Iron Curtain

Fear Not to Sow

In 1967, the W.H.O. offered a travelling fellowship to the Nursing Studies Department: it was W.H.O. policy at this time to encourage exchange visits between developed and underdeveloped countries, and the Nursing Studies Unit, with its links through the International School, was seen as a centre whose expertise should be shared. In spite of health problems, and colleagues therefore advising her against the tour, Elsie set her mind on going to study nursing services behind the Iron Curtain. Leaving Bill Gardner, whom she had married in 1964, was not easy for her either. Perhaps she already had some idea that her time was limited and that she should take this opportunity to round off her contribution to nursing.[1]

She was already thoroughly committed to the object of these W.H.O. Fellowships - to promote the international exchange of health knowledge and collaboration among health personnel. W.H.O. Fellows were expected to help spread awareness of each country's role in the welfare of the whole world, and of how the understanding and cooperation of each individual was vital.[2] Besides, she was eager to know at first hand what progress was being made in Yugoslavia where she had been thwarted in her wartime work, and in Poland, the home of many of her colleagues and patients from Bad Münder. Postcards from friends in Yugoslavia and Poland, written in 1962, urged her to come and see them again.[3]

"I would like to visit the equivalent of the British Ministry of Health of each country and the main Nursing Schools as well as University Centres of Medical and Social Sciences, Nursing Schools - advanced and basic - and service areas in Preventive Health and Sick Care...

As Director of the Department of Nursing Studies and the International School, I will be able to observe and discuss nursing and health care in the various countries. It would be invaluable in dealing with students from these countries and in comparing the varied health services and nursing education."[4]

She was granted leave of absence to observe nursing services and education programmes in U.S.S.R., Poland, Czechoslovakia, Yugoslavia and Turkey from 5th March to 21st April, 1967.

The tour would have been gruelling even for someone in the best of health: the first three weeks in Moscow and Riga, with daily visits to hospitals, schools of nursing, Red Cross centres, the Ministry of Health; a week in Warsaw making similar visits, giving talks, being interviewed by the B.B.C.; a week in Czechoslovakia, visiting centres in Prague, Kalin, and Brno; Yugoslavia for a week visiting Belgrade and Ljubljana; and finally a week in Turkey, where she divided her time between Ankara, Konya and Istanbul. On the return journey, she stopped off in Athens to meet associates from the Red Cross and discuss arrangements for the Florence Nightingale International Nursing Association Summer School at which she was to preside that September.

Throughout, she wrote regular detailed letters to Bill, as well as keeping a diary, in similar style to her wartime diaries - exact details of departure and arrival times, observations on the people she saw and met, the odd touch of humour, but little reflection or analysis. She did frequently record her feelings for Bill, but also her headaches, tiredness and nausea, and her need for religious comfort and strength.

Among the people she commented on in the U.S.S.R. were her companion and interpreter, Tanya, "a fair pleasant girl from the Ministry of Health"; the lady at the desk in her hotel "on duty 24 hours"; the hairdresser ("You'll laugh - the hairdresser said in Russian signs, I was like a Russian lady - the face, the hair and the build - then proceeded to point to my figure - and roars of laughter".[5] The women on duty at table at the Leningrad Hotel on Women's Day drew her comment, because men were supposed to do all the work in honour of women on that occasion. Others were "the children well wrapt (sic) up in fur coats and caps", the nurses and domestics in hospital working extra time due to staff shortages, the doctors who retired after 25 years on full pay "not like other medical workers - certainly a privileged class." "Great interest in Britain and many questions. My dear, I was told all from Britain would be welcome if they were like me!"[6] She chatted about collective farming, how families inherited their parents' wealth, and about the B.B.C. Wherever she went she was presented with dolls, flowers, mementos, which had to be parcelled up and sent home from time to time.

In Riga, after two hectic days spent visiting schools of nursing, paramedical schools, an ordinary flat, a cemetary, a cathedral, the old town and a ballet, she returned to her hotel room at midnight and was violently sick for two hours.

In spare moments during her stay in U.S.S.R. she was preparing the speech she had agreed to deliver in Warsaw.

"We are going to establish a University School of Nursing and we need as many arguments as possible to convince our opponents that the university nursing studies are really needed," the invitation letter had read.[7]

B.B.C. reporters, who were present at the lecture, arranged to interview her on Easter Saturday, and so she was able to record a message to Wincenty Tylmanowski and the Bad Münder patients for Polish radio.

Every waking moment during her week in Poland, she visited hospitals, health centres, and schools of nursing. She discussed university studies for nurses, talking to Old Internationals, some of whom had known very hard times during the war, and meeting people who planned to come and visit the Department in Edinburgh.

Czechoslovakia brought on a wave of homesickness, which she tried to combat by visiting a nearby Roman Catholic church. "I wanted to ring you last night," she wrote to Bill, "but resisted - tried to do as you said."[8] The country impressed her as being progressive and in many ways prosperous. She was vexed to learn, though, that the Rockefeller building, intended for nurses, had been taken over in 1948 for post-graduate medicine and never returned. Meetings with Old Internationals enlivened her evenings and visits. One visit to an obstetrics ward distressed her, when she learned that fathers were not allowed to see their wives and babes until three to four days after the birth, and then only in a special visitors' room away from the wards. Children in hospital here received no visits at all, she noted, except when dangerously ill.

As she moved from place to place, her luggage continued to increase. "I'm a bit like a Christmas tree getting into the plane. The wheels of the shopping bag are invaluable - hang all sorts on the handle and pull."[9]

Her return to Yugoslavia was emotional, and the excitement grew as she met old friends from wartime, and ex-students from Edinburgh. The status of the Chief Nurse, in charge of twelve types of paramedical personnel, impressed her so much that she wrote to Bill: "The room was at least the size of yours in the War Office - goodness, really in Chief position."[10]

Renewing old acquaintances, and learning about Yugoslavia twenty years after she had last seen it in disarray, kept her in a state of heightened emotion throughout this visit. She saw a film of the mountainous region, showing what health education had achieved there. She dined with ex-Partisans who had been involved in the organisation of the Yugoslav Red Cross. On one occasion she returned after a long day to find an ex-student waiting to see her at her hotel. *Very excited - and listened for some time - then just had to go to bed.*"[11]

Parties of nurses and Old Internationals seemed to happen around her, unannounced.

"They had cooked a real Slovene meal, and served in the traditional way, plus singing of international songs and Partisan songs. I shed tears - it brought back many happy and sad memories...My Serbo-Croat is very quickly coming back."[12]

Her send-off from Yugoslavia was memorable. A large number of friends turned up at the Red Cross to have coffee with her and give her presents before seeing her off. *A happy and fruitful stay in Yugoslavia - sorry to say goodbye.*"[13]

Friends in Yugoslavia had expressed concern about Elsie's projected visit to Turkey, and their premonitions were justified as soon as the journey began.

Arrived Istanbul 7.30 p.m...like Paddy's market - first passport control - then customs. Luggage grabbed - shouts for taxi, etc. -finally got my luggage upstairs...Back to check Ankara plane - told I had no booking. Waited a full hour before any information - during which time someone from American Express tried to get me into Israeli plane - not at all happy."[14]

This initial impression of Turkey set the tone of the rest of her stay there. People she was to visit had just left before she arrived, visits of interest to her had to be cut short due to lack of time, in Konya the car taking her to the Health Office ran out of petrol in the main street, and when she finally arrived at her destination the Medical Officer of Health was not there. In the nursing school no one was in uniform and all the students were away. One evening she gratefully sank into her bath, only to receive a phone call from the Medical Officer of Health asking her to come right away for further discussions. She took the opportunity to stress the importance of thorough nurse training.

When she did find a chance to talk to nurses, she found them very unsure of themselves, working in difficult situations, and with no advice on pay and conditions. In one school of nursing, run by doctors, student nurses were enrolled at the age of 15. Elsie found the whole situation very confused and the office "like paddy's market" as well. In another, she commented on the fact that men seemed to be in charge everywhere. "Needs a good woman to develope [sic] the school." One hospital she visited confirmed her misgivings about the lack of emphasis placed on nurse education. Intramuscular injections were being administered by untrained nursing aides, with scant regard for sterility, and the doctor who showed her round smoked all the time. The attitude prevailed that trained nurses were unnecessary. In another hospital, a system of first, second and third class beds was in operation, with camp beds provided in cases of severe overcrowding.

Highlights of the visit included lunch by the Bosphorus, and visits to the Florence Nightingale School in Istanbul, and then to Scutari where she saw the barracks and Florence Nightingale's room. *Thrilled to see this and to look from the window and imagine the situation.*"[15] The final trip to the airport rounded off the visit in typical fashion. "*A hair-raising trip...5-6 rows of traffic - carts, donkeys with milk cans, etc."*[16]

The stop in Athens, by contrast, was spent in happy anticipation of the Summer School of the Florence Nightingale International Nursing Association Conference in September. As President, Elsie had arrangements to make and people to meet. She was feted, photographed, her room was filled with carnations and roses. Prophetically and eerily, she scribbled amongst plans for the Summer School, some words from Byron's *The Isles of Greece:*

"Place me on Sunium's marbled steep,
Where nothing, save the waves and I,
May hear our mutual murmurs sweep;
There, swan-like, let me sing and die."

Chapter 12

The Wider View

Fear Not to Sow

However much energy her work absorbed, Elsie maintained a wide variety of interests, all related in some way to her view of the nurse's role in society.

The Royal Society of Health, an influential body in public health circles, bore obvious attractions for her, even though it was largely dominated by Medical Officers of Health and Sanitary Inspectors. This was the organisation which, until the Council for the Education and Training of Health Visitors took over in 1962, was responsible for the training of health visitors.[1] Normally the nursing contingent kept a low profile here, but Elsie was already making an impact at the Hastings Conference in 1953, when, as County Nursing Officer for Newcastle, she presented a paper on *The Application of Recent Research to Health Visiting.*

Not surprisingly, since nursing research was still at an early stage then, she was unable to quote many examples of recent research. She mentioned the Nuffield Foundation job analysis on nursing and public health, not yet published, and a World Health Organisation (W.H.O.) and Rockefeller Foundation study being carried out in England and France. She could talk about a small study she had carried out over the past year in Newcastle, examining the case load and job content of health visitors working in her area. Beyond that, she concentrated on consciousness-raising, picking out examples of the gap between hope and reality in nursing practice. In 1953, it was sufficiently remarkable to find a nurse bringing up such issues, in an atmosphere where many nurses had been so moulded by the establishment that they could not imagine any other situation, or were too diffident to voice their views.

"The work of the health visitor, if carried out conscientiously, is both comples, exacting and satisfying, and yet true fulfilment of her work is not always forthcoming and true recognition is often lacking. Is this due to the health visitor, to her early training, or to the lack of true understanding of the value of her work by those who plan and extend the services of the community?"

She raised issues which continue to exercise the minds of nurses and other health workers.

"Have we really sufficiently considered the possibility of the true nurse-student?"

"We go on increasing the variety of workers with very little real research. The health visitor, the midwife, the physiotherapist, the dietician, the almoner, etc., are all medical co-workers. Have we ever considered giving all this group a basic nursing course?"

"Are any of us satisfied with the type of record that is at present kept on many families?"

She quoted the introduction of general student nurses to the public health field, currently being undertaken in Newcastle. "The realisation that a patient in hospital has a home and family and the mental upset that is usually caused by hospitalisation has now at last been realised." The whole issue of the knowledge base for health visiting she dealt with in one sentence: "Are we any of us sure what the basic course needs to be for the key family worker?" She had publicly opened the windows of the institution of health visitor training, exposing a trail of dust and neglected tasks for all to see.

She maintained her links with the Royal Society of Health (R.S.H.), and by 1961, presenting her presidential address, this time in Blackpool, she lamented the fact that things had not changed as fast as she had hoped. In particular, the cooperation had not materialised which she had advocated between the various professionals dealing with the family. "Yet here we are in 1961, and still maintaining a separate Hospital Service, Family Doctor Service, Local Health Authority Service and Dental Service. We may well ask the question. Why?" In spite of her belief that hospitals were merely a small part of the health service, hospitalisation continued to increase, and expenditure favoured hospitals over community services.

"We learn that a greater amount of money has been set aside for our hospital service - but what of the preventive health service? Have we any? How many health centres have we built? How much money has been devoted to demonstrating and evaluating health visiting and home nursing care? What have we done to reduce morbidity rates?"

Her vision of a revolutionised nurse education had still not come to fruition. "The first nursing college, coordinating the health and social aspects of the individual, sick and well, is still awaited."

Despite the august nature and the male domination of the R.S.H., Elsie managed to make an impression. The fact that the men had the power does not seem to have concerned her in the least. In 1960, when the Health Visitor Section was discussing the role of men in health visiting, she scribbled on her copy of the report: "Let us get away from this idea that the study and care of man is only for women and not for men."

She made her feelings plain, too, when bureaucracy acted against her. On moving to Scotland in 1956, she had resigned from her role as recording secretary, in accordance with a regulation on residence qualifications. She was invited to be recording secretary at the Eastbourne Conference in 1965, and her reply gives an insight into her means of coping with conflict.

"Regarding resignations, I am surprised and angry at what you have said, as in 1956, I was advised that it would be necessary for me to resign my position on taking up residence in Scotland. I am, however, glad that this is no longer so."[2]

Through the R.S.H., she was able to have some nursing influence on the economic and political considerations affecting health care. It made sense, therefore, when she suggested for the 1965 conference the topic: *Politics in Nursing,* with a professor of politics and a nurse as speakers. Mr. Robert Maxwell, publisher, and at that time Member of Parliament, with whom Elsie had connections through Pergamon Press, agreed to preside at the public health nursing section.

"The theme...has nothing to do directly with political parties. It is concerned with the art and science of government and its influence on the nursing service. For example, the importance of administration, the allocation of funds; the role of the nursing officer - has she the freedom to present her own reports to various levels of the administration, etc."[3]

In preparation for his address to the conference, Elsie sent Robert Maxwell background notes, many of which were reflected or repeated in his speech. As there were still few research results on which to base reasoned arguments, Elsie's position and reputation gave her power to state her opinions as facts, and to influence others to think like her. Mr. Maxwell spoke of the need to attract first class minds into nursing, of the importance of cooperation between hospital and home, of the nurse's unique role in preventive health, of the need to imporve the status of nursing by means of improved educational provision, and of the advisability of nurses joining trade unions to improve pay and conditions.[4]

While Mr. Maxwell was under no obligation to adopt any of Elsie's suggestions as the basis for his speech, the fact that he did so illustrates Elsie's persuasive influence. Her connections with the R.S.H. continued until her death, and her last appearance in public was at one of the society's conferences.[5]

The Florence Nightingale International Nursing Association was also a natural home for someone with Elsie's leanings, founded as it was on Mary Adelaide Nutting's proposal for an international research-based study centre for nurses, with emphasis on the kindred problems of hospitals and public health.[6] Elsie, of all people, was interested in the "kindred problems of hospitals and public health", and in bringing about international understanding among nurses. She was proud of belonging to the Old Internationals, composed of the Association scholarship winners, and through it she made contacts all over the world, notably during her last tour for the W.H.O.

Her interest continued throughout her years in East Suffolk and then in Newcastle where she was involved in the idea of a reunion of Old Internationals, at which the group would study "the value of a shared professional training with its ethical standards as an influence for peace."[7] For various reasons, the reunion was postponed, and it was not until 1964 that the Summer School did take place at Holland House, an Edinburgh University Hall of Residence. Elsie was a moving force in the organisation of the event, as well as in the recognition accorded by the City of Edinburgh, where the grass plot on the Mound displayed a floral emblem of the Lamp, and the Castle was floodlit for the occasion.[8] It may not have come as too much of a surprise, therefore, when her nomination as President went unopposed.

Her 1965 Presidential Address to the Association reflects the pressure under which she was still working in Edinburgh:

"If she (Florence Nightingale) and many of her followers were among us today...would they not be castigating the rigid conservatism which binds itself to all that is happening in and around the world in which nurses are called to serve."

In the ever-changing world to today, Elsie argued, there was a growing need for well-educated nurses who would be able to keep the profession abreast of new developments. The aims of the Florence Nightingale International Fellowship should enable its members to "build into the life of the world a living memorial to her whose pioneering spirit and indomitable will laid the foundation for all modern nursing."

By the following year's Presidential Address, she was able to quote a few advances in the status of nursing, such as the University of Surrey's acceptance of a nursing component to a degree course. But still she felt her profession needed awakening to advances in science and technology.

"I am saddened when I see so many amongst our leaders who seem unconscious of the facts of the world in which we live, and of the aids and opportunities it is developing for extending and improving in a multitude of ways the services which we nurses seek to give to mankind, from cradle to grave. Eyes are often closed and minds shut to the breadth and depth of nursing - we have stood still too long."

She urged her audience to "be zealous missionaries, and expand your vision of the part the nurse should play in developing the civilisation of today and tomorrow."

September, 1967, was the date for the Florence Nightingale International Nursing Association Summer School in Athens, when Elsie was to preside. Her health had prevented her from returning to work after the tour of the Iron Curtain countries. Bill wrote to the Summer School Annual General Meeting, describing the disappointment they had both felt when Elsie's health began to raise doubts about her fitness to travel to Greece. "Even so, she continued to hope, up to a week or ten days before her death, that she would recover in time to be with you all in Athens."[9] Three days before her death in July, 1967, she wrote to the Iona Community, asking for a St. John Cross on an Iona marble base to be sent to the Chapel of the Greek Red Cross Society.

For the past two years, she had been sending small donations to Florence Nightingale House to fund a room there on behalf of the Nursing Studies Department and the International School of Nursing. After Elsie's death, Miss Kathleen Wilson, of the Nursing Studies Department, and Miss Craven of Florence Nightingale House, agreed between them that the plaque on the room should include "Director, Elsie Stephenson, M.A., S.R.N., S.C.M., H.V. Cert., F.R.S.H. 1956-67."

Elsie had been very much one of the Old Internationals, whose influence was at its peak between the two wars. By sending nurses on public health courses, to study and live together, the Florence Nightingale Association not only created an opportunity for the public health field to develop, but also formed a nucleus of public health nurses who were friends and international colleagues. The confidence and status provided by such an organisation are inestimable, and Elsie throughout her life was devoted to spreading the spirit of the Florence Nightingale International Nursing Association.

Elsie's membership of the Soroptimists went back to her time as County Nursing Officer in Newcastle, when she and her friend Margaret Freeman joined together. Margaret remembers club meetings as interesting times when a diverse body of women came together to exchange views, creating a refreshing relief from the closed world of nursing. Elsie used the opportunity to make links with people who might in some way help her in her work and once these contacts were made, she never neglected them.

Among the Soroptimists, Elsie had once more found her niche in an organisation of women which dated back to the years immediately after the First World War, and with aims in tune with her own:

"To promote a free and responsible society in which women take an active part in decision-making at all levels...to advance the status of women...to foster understanding among women throughout the world."[10]

Elsie did not feel the need to become strident about women's rights in the nursing profession. Her early struggles with her conscience and her family had built in her a quiet confidence, and her contacts in the nursing world and such organisations as the Red Cross and the Florence Nightingale International Nursing Association reinforced her conviction that women and men had equal roles to play in society. She seldom felt the need to argue the point; this basic assurance in her own status may have been the strongest factor in her favour, both in achieving the post of Director of the Nursing Studies Unit, and in winning for the Unit the recognition and respect which soon grew, in university as well as in nursing circles.

Once installed in the University of Edinburgh, Elsie naturally became interested in the publication of nursing material. Her connections with Pergamon Press began in the early 1960s, when she became Divisional Editor for Nursing in the Commonwealth and International Library.

Shortly after this connection had been made, in 1963, she founded and edited the *International Journal of Nursing Studies,* also published by Pergamon Press.[11] After her death, the Journal devoted an article to Elsie, in which the Editor paid tribute to her "strong belief that nursing could play a valuable part in promoting international understanding."[12]

The other two journals with which she was connected were *Midwife and Health Visitor*, of which she was editorial adviser, and *Medical Care*, where she was a member of the Editorial Board. She was a fund of ideas for these journals, even if her success in bringing her ideas to fruition was not always noteworthy. For *Midwife and Health Visitor*, she began to collect a series of profiles of eminent nurses, but found that many were somewhat retiring, and unwilling to have themselves publicised for the purposes of the journal.

Elsie had little time for such reticence in her own dealings with editors and journal owners. After agreeing to join the editorial board of *Midwife and Health Visitor* she investigated the possibility of using her fee of 100 guineas per annum towards setting up a Chair of Nursing at Edinburgh University. Occasionally, she would find herself committed to writing articles which she had suggested, when no-one else could be found to carry out the work. For *Midwife and Health Visitor,* for instance, she was asked to produce an editorial at very short notice. In the space of five days, she produced a piece on the subject, "Are our midwives and health visitors less well prepared than primary school teachers? These are the teachers of the mothers of the future and instructors in health." As was becoming more and more her wont, she asked many rhetorical questions, which in a speech might have prodded people into action by the discomfort produced, but were merely inconclusive when written down. On such occasions, it was becoming apparent that, although Elsie had the will to blow a wind of change through nursing, she had neither the academic ability nor the research backing to convince people by reasoning of the validity of her claims. She seldom had any such problems when confronted with an audience, when her charisma swept all before her.

The editorial was rejected. The editor wrote to her, "I felt it rather difficult to build on it as it seemed to suggest that Midwives and Health Visitors were, at present, inadequately trained for their task, but made no suggestion as to how this could be remedied."[13] Two days later, Elsie sent back a hurt little note: "I am sorry that you felt unable to use the Editorial, as I felt that it was very clear regarding what must be done to remedy the situation; that is, not to accept people without an adequate education in the first place." This from Elsie was ironic indeed, given her own precarious educational position.

Medical Care, which started publication early in 1963, aimed "to deal with every aspect of medical care - now a leading domestic problem in every country." The advertising material claimed that this would be the first journal of its kind in the world. Clearly Elsie would feel proud to see her name snuggling modestly among the list of eminent members of the editorial board. She was the only woman among ten professors and four doctors.

At the first Steering Committee meeting, held in London on 4th July, 1962, Elsie was one of the five representatives of the Board in attendance. Fragments of correspondence suggest a touch of acrimony between Professor Brotherston of the Usher Institute in Edinburgh and Elsie, over this matter. "After discussion with my colleagues it has been decided that I should attend the first meeting of the Steering Committee." wrote Elsie to Dr. Marcus, Editor of *Medical Care.*[14]

To Dr. Brotherston, the tone was explanatory, but not apologetic.

"I would like to point out that I did not offer to go as representative at this first meeting of the Editorial Board of *Medical Care.* The other members of the group have asked me to represent them. If you would prefer to make other arrangements I should be only too happy to cooperate."[15]

In any event she went to the meeting, perhaps more determined than ever to assert her views. One of the possible contributions discussed was the education of nurses. "Miss Stephenson put the situation that exists now - our nurses failing to get posts abroad because of inferior educational standards. Miss Stephenson is writing about this."[16] The Editor's suggestion for the article was "Something in the region of 2,000 words...If it is possible to include tables as Professor Backett suggested, it would be an advantage.

By the middle of October, he was once more urging her to produce the promised article, as time was getting short. She finally submitted it on 2nd November, by which time, the Editor's response was a very polite rejection. "I am afraid it won't be possible to fit it into the first number of 'Medical Care,' but I hope I may be able to include it in the second. But I think it needs some revision - it should be a little more closely argued and the figures would be essential."[17]

The article, entitled *Nursing Today and Tomorrow,* is an indication of how harassed Elsie was at that time, and how short on sound academic advice. It is easy to criticise the article for lack of figures and diagrams, although she does briefly mention the Nuffield Provincial Hospitals Trust *Report on The Work of Nurses in Hospital Wards,* (London, 1953). What had perhaps not occurred to the magazine editor, or the medical profession in general, was that precious few figures were available to her for referral, and very little nursing research had been done. Elsie was aware of this herself, although it seems likely that she did not begin to appreciate the amount of time, money and patience that would be required to build up enough data for someone in her position to produce the quality of magazine article that the editor was apparently seeking.

For all that, her article betrays some astonishing insights and prophetic statements, hinting at the remarkable intelligence and foresight behind her somewhat amateurish attempt at producing an article. "Undoubtedly we need re-organisation, even federation ofthe varied recognised statutory nursing bodies," she states, some twenty years in advance of the establishment of the United Kingdom Central Council for Nursing, Midwifery and Health Visiting (the UKCC). She defines the responsibility of the nurse, "to initiate and develop the total nursing care of the patient", again twenty years in advance of the profession's adoption of the nursing process. "Far too many doctors look upon the nurse only as a pair of hands; she is, in reality, a working colleague with full access to a wealth of untapped and potential material," she wrote. This was well in advance of the years when the profession would talk of the nurse practitioner and nursing diagnosis. The spirit of her message is clear enough, and her vision shines through.

Medical Care was published in Britain until the end of 1966, when its consistent failure to make a profit forced its sale to Lippincotts in the United States. Elsie wrote to the Editor at the magazine's demise: "I have felt some disappointment in it over a period as there has been so little published on nursing."[18] She had done her best, but her own shortcomings, and the lack of back up from her own profession had contributed to this small failure. *The International Journal of Nursing Studies*, however, continues to be published.

Elsie's other major interests were several. She maintained connections with church, youth clubs, the Epilepsy Association of Edinburgh, and the Red Cross, as Chief Nursing Officer of the Edinburgh Branch until she died.

Chapter 13

Private Life

Fear Not to Sow

It is almost impossible to separate Elsie's private life from her career, so thoroughly were the two intertwined. Deep and lasting friendships were born during training days, and throughout her life colleagues were included in the Stephenson family circle. Margaret Freeman, a friend from training days at the West Suffolk General Hospital, recalls the camping holidays she shared with Elsie:

"The first year we went in the tent I didn't think she was serious. I thought the idea was we would have the tent in case we couldn't get fixed up anywhere. But not on your sweet life. We camped in this tent, and the pair of us got in with a shoe horn, I think."

The dogs went with them, and Elsie slept with a baton under her pillow for self defence.

But whereas her friends on camping holidays tended to use the opportunity to switch off completely from the nursing scene, Elsie would never miss a chance to go and visit the local hospital or make some useful professional contact. Similarly, she often became personally involved in matters which others might have regarded as professional. While in Singapore and North Borneo, she paid for supplies and equipment out of personal expenses, just to set things moving. In Ljubljana, she shed tears "so touched by everything - brought back old memories."[1] Nowhere in Elsie's attitude to nursing was there a straining after personal detachment.

There was nothing saintly about her, for all that. Elsie's friends remember her as being tremendous fun to be with, a real extrovert, the life and soul of the party. Her diaries are not those of someone with a bent for profound reflection and analysis. Her assurance in circumstances which were, to say the least, uncertain suggests that she was not someone who spent much time soul-searching. Yet she could be deeply serious when the occasion demanded it. She told Bill that hers was a "simple faith", and this must surely be where she drew her strength. Some people who knew her very well realised the importance religion played in Elsie's life. In general, however, she kept her religious beliefs to herself, and expressed them through action rather than preaching. The moments she spent in church and in prayer replenished her resources of wisdom and courage enough to see her through some very difficult times.

One of the few occasions when she spoke publicly about her beliefs was when she addressed a Conservative Nurses' meeting:

"I am a nurse. I wanted to be a nurse from the time that I was old enough to have any conscious amount of understanding. I belong to no political party, but I am much concerned with politics - inasmuch as I am much concerned with people and the conditions under which they have to live and work."[2]

This is an excellent summary of Elsie's approach to her life and work.

She was notorious for her cooking methods, the philosophy of which was "waste not, want not". Friends insist that the end product was usually enjoyable, if unpredictable. Once, for instance, out of a tin of salmon, some leftover porridge from breakfast, a few carrots and peas, she produced two delicious salmon moulds. On another occasion, a friend enjoying a beef stew made by Elsie came across a fish bone. When challenged about this anomaly in her beef stew, Elsie grinned and said, "Oh, you would be the one to find it."

Her extraordinary energy allowed her to make the most of any time off. Audrey Atherton, a lifelong friend, remembers going from Northumberland to visit Elsie in Edinburgh. When Sunday turned out bright, Elsie suggested to the family a trip to the Trossachs. The Athertons said they realised she was a busy person and that she was not to trouble herself on their behalf. "Get away," said Elsie. "I've already done the washing." And so off they went for the day, and she went into work the next day, full of energy.

One of her many contradictions was her overwhelming generosity, which contrasted with her parsimony in the kitchen. She always brought gifts home from abroad for her friends, and she gave with a kind of intoxicating joy. Audrey Atherton's children were given rocking horses, desks, their first puppy, a tortoise, which Elsie held hidden under her coat when she arrived on one of her visits. While in Turkey, during the W.H.O. tour, she discovered it was the 31st birthday of one of her companions. "Gave her my gold modern brooch", she records in her diary. In 1956, amid the upheaval of her removal to Edinburgh, she contacted the Red Cross, offering to take a Hungarian refugee child. The offer was not taken up, however, since most children were in family groups, and the aim was to keep them together.[3]

For clothes, she had little taste, and would buy on impulse when she knew she needed a new outfit. Sometimes her presents suffered from the same impulsiveness. One Christmas she gave everybody checked gaiters, some bright red, some bottle green.

Heidi, the au pair to Elsie's mother, remembers how Elsie was always in a hurry and never had time to worry about her appearance. When Elsie had to go out for a party or a special occasion at the university: "Usually I had to give her dress a good brushing (and quick) and off she hurried. She never bothered about a hole in her stockings or a loose strap on her petticoat."[4]

Often, before she had to give a speech, she would rush out and buy a new hat. That was the only outward sign of any nervousness provoked by such occasions. She would keep a few notes on cards, but simply stand up and speak in front of any audience. Her delivery was confident, simple, and always inspiring.

Many people who met through Elsie have remained lifelong friends. Margaret Freeman, Elsie's nursing friend, and Audrey Atherton, who had known Elsie from the days when the family farmed at Crawleas, remain close friends. One of their memories of Elsie is her love of practical jokes.

She held on to all her contacts, and made use of them. Students in need of work abroad would be referred to some personal contact of Elsie's. Her privacy does not appear to have mattered to her. She genuinely loved people, and needed them around her.

Since her religious beliefs, her career and her private life were so closely entwined, examples of how she juggled the various aspects are numerous. Many of her friends remember with joy the evening when she invited Indonesian students studying at Newcastle to perform a ritual candle dance during one of the soirees at her home.

Her mother, disabled by a stroke, and dependent for most of her needs, lived with Elsie in Newcastle and Edinburgh. Heidi, the Swiss au pair, became a close friend of Elsie's, managed to win over the mother, and generally enabled Elsie to continue with her career. Whenever possible, Elsie would take her mother and Heidi with her on trips connected with her work. Sometimes she would come home on a summer's evening, pack the evening meal into the car and take them both to the seaside for a picnic. In both Newcastle and Edinburgh, Elsie's mother and her wheelchair often accompanied her on professional outings. Many people retain great respect for the way Elsie handled a situation which might well have drained her strength and inner resources.

The other side of this coin is that it cannot have been easy to work with Elsie. She threw herself into her work with such energy and dedication, and was so willing to forgo any private life, that few colleagues must have felt ready to match her single-mindedness. For all that, she did surround herself with excellent staff, endowed with a great variety of qualities (such as academic ability, quiet application to the task in hand, bringing ideas down to the practical level) that Elsie herself did not possess.

Elsie's brother, Harry, has no memory of Elsie ever wanting marriage and children. In fact, the general impression in the family was that the mother did not want her children married, but hoped they would stay with her. Naturally, this applied to the only girl even more forcefully than to the three boys. Audrey Atherton remembers how Elsie had plenty of male company when she was young. Her brothers' friends were always around the house, and the parties at the Stephenson house in Newmarket were renowned. Only one friend, Jack, might have been special, but he was killed in the war. Nothing among Elsie's papers suggests she suffered any great emotional trauma at that death. The impression is that she had no time for marriage and children. Margaret Freeman recalls she would say to suitors, "Ask me in eight years. I haven't time."

It, therefore, came as something of a bombshell when, not long after her mother died, she announced her engagement to Bill Gardner. When she told her friends she was thinking of getting married, they asked who the lucky man was. "Someone from the War Office, from London" was the standard reply. They imagined some pin-stripe clad, smart, civil servant, and were all amazed, when they met him, to find that Bill was a plump elderly man, 21 years Elsie's senior.

Knowing how she had cared for her mother, friends speculated that Elsie had only laid down one burden to take up another, and that she would soon be nursing Bill through his old age. Some friends continued to feel, after the marriage, that all the fun had gone from knowing Elsie. She and Bill spent all their spare time together, and there were no more camping holidays with friends. Others saw the marriage as a source of great comfort and happiness for Elsie during the most exacting years of her life.

After their initial meeting at the International Red Cross Conference in Stockholm in 1948, the friendship between Bill and Elsie continued to grow over the years. Bill reserved seats at the War Office for Elsie and her mother for the Coronation in 1953,[5] and Mrs. Stephenson was heard to mutter that "that fellow has designs on our Elsie," but no one else seems to have put any such construction on the friendship.

"I do not think either of us ever doubted that we met and our friendship developed because it was God's purpose for us," Bill wrote later. Dame Elizabeth Cockayne, former Chief Nursing Officer at the Ministry of Health, and a close friend of Elsie's, remembers that "when she told me that she was going to marry Bill Gardner she remarked that she would do it when she had time!"

Any reader of this biography of Elsie who did not know her personally, will by this stage be wondering who is this Bill Gardner and what has he been doing throughout Elsie's busy life? An extract from '*Who's Who*' gives the bare outline of the man. William Henry Gardner had been Assistant Under-Secretary of State. Born on 20th April, 1895, he had joined the Civil Service as an Assistant Clerk in the Board of Education in 1912, and had worked his way to Second

146

Division Clerk in the War Office by the time the First World War broke out. He served with the Queen's Westminster Rifles throughout the war before returning to a Minor Staff Clerk post in 1919, three years after Elsie's birth. Gradually he rose through the ranks until he was appointed Chairman of the Inter-Departmental Committee on the revision of the Prisoners of War and Red Cross Conventions and the Maritime Convention, from 1947-49. In June, 1948, he was awarded the C.M.G. He was also Deputy Leader of the United Kingdom Delegation to the International Convention for the Protection of War Victims in Geneva from April to August, 1949. In August of 1951 he represented the War Office at the African Facilities Conference in Nairobi, became Assistant Under-Secretary of State on 1st May, 1952, and was awarded the Coronation Medal in 1953.

The engagement announcement in *The Scotsman* in August, 1964, raised speculation among nursing colleagues in Edinburgh about whether this would be the end of Elsie's career. It soon became apparent, however, even to those who did not understand the depth of the relationship between Bill and Elsie, that she intended nothing to change in her career. Students were occasionally known to refer to the couple as "Mr. and Mrs. Stephenson", so thoroughly did Bill become involved in Elsie's life. He left his own home in Walthamstow to move up to Edinburgh with her, and soon he was spending much of his time at the Department of Nursing Studies, and helping with entertaining students at home. Students knew him as Bill, and he knew most of them by name. Only at church was she Mrs. Gardner. Otherwise, she was still Miss Stephenson, or Mrs. Stephenson Gardner, a title which caused confusion when she was planning her W.H.O. tour in 1967.

The wedding took place on the 14th November, 1964, at St. Michael's Church, Cornhill, London, and was conducted by the Venerable Archdeacon of Southend, Neville Welch. Margaret Freeman was Maid of Honour and John Payling of Walthamstow was Best Man. Photographs show Elsie wearing an expression of deepest solemnity, strangely out of tune with her reputation as the carefree life and soul of the party. A similar expression on an early photograph of her as a newly-qualified nurse shows her profound sense of occasion.

The most touching memorial of how much this marriage meant to them both is to be found in the letters Elsie sent to Bill from Russia. She was unwell by this time, and almost constantly suffering from headaches. A typical comment in her letters: "A mixed night - a bit of a nightmare - no you - read Father Andrew and calmed down." In a happier mood, she wrote to him about an encounter in Russia:

"Coming up from the beach, I spoke to three old ladies sitting on a seat - they were so happy that I spoke to them and one asked me how my husband let me come away without him - was he not afraid he would lose me - I said no - we loved each other. That I hoped one day I could bring him to this lovely spot and they might meet him."

From Poland on Easter Sunday, "You will now be getting ready to go to St. Columba's. I will be with you."

In November, 1965, she had undergone a mastectomy for breast cancer, but was declared fit to go on her tour of eastern European countries. Her last illness, therefore, took most people by surprise. On her return from the W.H.O. tour, she was said to be suffering from a chest infection, and was admitted to hospital. Few people realised the gravity of the illness, although Elsie herself knew she had not long to live. One of her notebooks contains a pencilled list of her possessions and who should inherit them in the event of her death. When Margaret Auld visited her in her flat shortly before her death, she found Bill and Elsie at the kitchen table, labelling meat to be frozen in packs for one person - for Bill's use after she was gone.

Bill wanted to surround Elsie with quiet during her illness, and friends had difficulty finding out from him how to contact her. Margaret Freeman and Audrey Atherton determined to make the journey anyway.

"When we got there what a welcome we got. She had told them she wouldn't need the ambulance that afternoon to go for her deep X-ray. She had told them her friend would take her...She was like a different person. She blossomed with people, couldn't live without them."[6]

She died on 16th July, 1967. Having dedicated her life to the service of mankind, she left her body for medical research. Bill took her final remains to be buried at Walthamstow, with the inscription:

"Praise God for the life of Elsie Gardner (nee Stephenson).

First Director of Nursing Studies, University of Edinburgh, 1956-67.

President, Florence Nightingale International Nursing Association, 1966-67.

Fellow, Royal Society of Health, 1956-67.

British Red Cross Society, 1946-67.

Born 22nd January, 1916. Died 16th July, 1967. Ashes interred 5th October, 1969. R.I.P."

At the memorial service for her in St. Mary's Cathedral, Edinburgh, on 1st November, 1967, the address delivered by Miss J. Elsie Gordon celebrated the joy of Elsie's life. "This occasion should not be regarded as entirely mournful. We are, rather, recognising with pride the achievements of a woman with great courage and ability."

Chapter 14

Elsie's Lamp

Fear Not to Sow

"Monuments to the glory of God are not only of bricks and mortar".[1]

In any evaluation of Elsie Stephenson's place in nursing history, it is tempting to think only in terms of her achievements at Edinburgh University. But it would be unjust to forget what she achieved as a health visitor, and as a nurse with a belief in her teaching role among the sick and homeless and destitute in the Second World War, and as a woman who refused to allow her work to be overlooked or devalued simply because it was the unglamorous role of caring for people.

One of her most disarming features was the fact that she never lost sight of the humble task that nurses choose, out of a loving desire to help others.

"All intending nurses have love in their hearts for men - we must develop this, kindle and train it - for service to man himself."[2]

On this foundation she aimed to build her own monument to the glory of God. No matter how one views the work she did at Edinburgh, and the heritage she left behind her, there can be little debate about her success as an ordinary nurse and a citizen of the world.

The immediate response to the question: "What did Elsie achieve?" tends, therefore, to be that her achievements and her influence were personal. People who worked with her remember her cheerfulness, her warmth, her sincerity.

Students remember how she inspired them, made them believe in themselves, helped them achieve more than they ever thought they could, opened their minds to a whole world of knowledge. Margaret Brayton, Executive Secretary of the Commonwealth Nurses Federation, continues to meet nurses in senior posts throughout the Commonwealth who talk in glowing terms of Elsie.

"Their memories are very vivid of those days in Edinburgh, and so long as they are in charge in their respective lands, Elsie's 'lamp' will continue to shine in their sometimes difficult environment."[3]

Throughout her career, testimonials referred to her outstanding care for her patients. The devotion with which she cared for her mother was example enough of the art and science of nursing at its highest.

Two outstanding qualities fitted Elsie for the difficult situation she faced in Edinburgh. The first was her willingness to re-evaluate everything in nursing from first principles. In the 1960s, this was fashionable and popular with students and some academics, while nurses in Scotland tended to be cautious and hidebound. Elsie promised to blow a wind of change through the nursing world. This was her great attraction.

This was also what worried many senior nurses in Scotland, and where Elsie's second outstanding quality came into play. She had an amazing ability to resolve conflict. Elsie's apprenticeship in diplomacy went back as far as the days when she had learned to reconcile her determination to nurse with her profound need to be a dutiful daughter. Throughout her career, she had been learning how to achieve her aims through cooperation rather than confrontation. "The best little fraterniser in Yugoslavia," a friend had called her. "Fear not to sow because of the birds," she had scribbled in a notebook in Toronto.

And so one sees her grasping the nettle in public, first in an address to nurse tutors in 1963:

"First, may I pay tribute to your past president, Miss Margaret Lamb, the R.C.N. (Scottish Branch), who has served you and nursing so well. Miss Lamb has always been a keen supporter and worker for University education for nurses, and assisted in the early development of the Unit...Nursing in all its spheres is a key social service. Throughout its history it has been fraught with emotions, and personal loyalties to a few leaders has often split our profession. We need to cooperate in the interests of the profession, and for those we serve, to promote what is good and eliminate what is bad. The courage and enthusiasm required from each of you needs to be transferred to your students."[4]

On another occasion, she talked of conflict and how to deal with it:

"Conflicts are inevitable between human beings. Do not be afraid of them. What matters is how we deal with them, and the kind of atmosphere we create...Make people feel the real friendliness and warmth generally called human relationships."[5]

The ability to look disharmony straight in the eye typified Elsie's methods of disarming her critics.

Anyone who had entered the post of Director of Nursing Studies at Edinburgh University with all the drawbacks in mind could have been forgiven for feeling somewhat daunted. Elsie appears to have had no such doubts. As one senior nurse put it, "Elsie batted on", proving that it was possible to "take your courage in both hands, move into an unfamiliar environment and manage to get something established."[6]

And here we find another of Elsie's qualities which helped her to pioneer the Nursing Studies Unit as successfully as she did. Her confidence and persuasiveness swept all before her. Where others might have stopped to wonder or analyse, Elsie forged ahead, her head full of wonderful ideas and schemes, for which she never attempted to work out the details. If ever there was a time for a visionary nurse, it was in Edinburgh in the 1960's.

How long Elsie would have been able to continue to hold the post of Director of Nursing Studies is debatable. Some of her closest friends feel that she would soon have recognised her own limitations in the academic field, and, having fulfilled the pioneering role at which she excelled, she would have left the post open to someone more academically qualified. Dr. Margaret Scott Wright, Elsie's successor to the directorship, and ultimately Britain's first Professor of Nursing, was highly equipped in many of those areas where Elsie was weak. Dr. Scott Wright had obtained her doctorate at Edinburgh University and had been Matron of the Middlesex Hospital in London.

Miss Annie Altschul, now Emeritus Professor of Nursing, who joined the Nursing Studies Department in Elsie's time, and became a leading figure in the international nursing scene as well as Professor of Nursing at Edinburgh after Professor Scott Wright, was called upon to evaluate the Nursing Studies Department at her retiring dinner in 1983.[7] She spoke of the general concensus in university circles that students on the nursing courses brought a new and challenging dimension to the life of the university. Departments had been known to complain if there were no nurses in their classes for a particular year. Elsie's insistence from the beginning that all nurses on courses at the Unit should attend at least one course from the general university syllabus had borne fruit.

There can be no disputing the contribution that the Department of Nursing Studies has continued to make to the sum of nursing knowledge, to which the large range of published material and research papers emanating from the department bear witness. The opportunity for able men and women to fulfil a caring role in society while meeting the intellectual challenges presented by the life of a university has been grasped and greatly appreciated by many people. The Nursing Studies Department and its staff, and the Nursing Research Unit, continue to act as consultants to the nursing profession both in the United Kingdom and abroad.

While Elsie had never entertained any doubts that the job of nursing deserved the very best brains, and that the most excellent education should be available for nurses, the debate about university education for nurses has continued. In the late 1970s, W.H.O. registered its support for more university programmes for nurses at both undergraduate and postgraduate level:

"...in the belief that the better educated nurse is able to function more effectively in diverse service situations and to provide quality care to larger groups of people...It is time that the protracted and frequently misinformed debate on whether nursing should be taught at academic level be closed: the pattern is now accepted as both necessary and desirable."[8]

Elsie carried out her role of ventilating stale areas in the nursing world, thereby allowing the wind of change to blow through, with panache. Her skills of oratory were enhanced by her genius for annexing the wisdom of others, and her lecture notes are peppered with quotations from great thinkers:

"A poor man served by thee shall make thee rich;
A rich man served by thee shall make thee strong;
Thou shalt be served thyself by every sense
Of service which though renderest." (Robert Browning)[9]

"The noblest of all studies is what man is and how we should live." (Plato)[10]

"I like the idea of a healthy nation, a healthy world - not purely physical, but in spirit, in body and in mind," she told health visitors at their Centenary celebrations in June, 1962, decades before the W.H.O. campaigns aimed at *Health for All by the Year 2000.* In line with her beliefs, nurse education for the future in Great Britain aims at a Common Foundation Programme for student nurses based on health and not on illness, and at a better balance between hospital and community experience.[11]

Her vision of the essential role of nursing in the search for healthy living allowed her to enter with confidence into other fields beyond the immediate. In Newcastle she made her mark on the Women's Civic Committee. She served as a representative on the Council of Edinburgh University Settlement Association. "She wanted to embrace the whole world," Margaret Freeman said of her.[12] Elsie would undoubtedly have approved the presence of two nurses, Baroness Cox and Baroness Macfarlane, in the House of Lords. Although she declared herself to belong to no political party, she was aware that, as a nurse, she had knowledge that ought to be used in the decision-making processes of her country.

"For too long in this country nursing has been treated as the poor relation of uncle medicine...We need our nurse researchers, teachers, administrators at every level".[13]

Yet she did not wish nurses to threaten the role of doctors; simply that nursing should be given full status as a distinct profession, with practitioners just as qualified as for any other profession. A confident, assertive woman, she adopted and promoted one of woman's most traditional, caring and downgraded roles. As such, she should take her place among the advocates of woman's right to carry her lamp into often neglected and shrouded places.*

Opening session of the FNINA Conference in September, 1967, at which Elsie was to have presided.

NOTES

Abbreviations: The initials ESC in any of the following notes refers to the Elsie Stephenson Collection, located in the Medical Archive Centre, of the University of Edinburgh, Scotland, the staff of which are gratefully acknowledged for their unstinting aid to the author.

Chapter One
1. David Shermer, *World War I*, Octopus Books, 1973.
2. Newmarket Grammar School Records.
3. Florence Nightingale International Nursing Association (FNINA) *Newsletter*, unsigned, Profile of Elsie Stephenson, 1965.
4. Brian Abel-Smith, *A History of the Nursing Profession,* Heinemann Educational Books Ltd., 1960.
5. Margaret Freeman to Sheila Allan, 17.4.84.
6. B. Abel-Smith, *Op. cit.*
7. Elsie Stephenson Collection (ESC), Medical Archive Centre, University of Edinburgh, Box 20.
8. M. Freeman's Obituary about Elsie for West Suffolk General Hospital Appeal.
9. B. Abel-Smith, *Op. cit.*
10. *Ibid.*
11. *Ibid.*
12. *Ibid.*
13. *Ibid*.
14. Agnes Scott to William Gardner, ESC.
15. Joyce Double to S. Allan, 14.11.84.
16. Jenny Causer to W. Gardner, Memories of Midwifery Training, 1.7.38 to 21.6.39.
17. *Ibid.*
18. Margaret Vaughan Jones to W. Gardner, 10.11.68.
19. J. Double to S. Allan, Op. cit.
20. Elaine Wilkie, *A Singular Anomaly,* Royal College of Nursing, 1984, pp. 13-19.
21. B. Abel-Smith, *Op. cit.*

Chapter Two
1. Dr. H. Rogers to W. Gardner, 2.1.69.
2. Lucy R. Seymer, *A General History of Nursing,* Faber & Faber, London, 1961.

3. County Medical Officer, West Suffolk County Council, 24.1.44.

4. *Ibid.*

5. L. R. Seymer, *Op. cit.*

6. Peter King,(undated) *Twentieth Century British History Made Simple,* W. H. Allen.

7. Elsie Stephenson, Paper entitled "The Scope and Limitations of the Almoner's Case Work Contribution to the Total Care of the Patient", 1956.

8. Elsie Stephenson's address to the Conference celebrating the 100th anniversary of health visiting in London, 1962.

9. Elsie Stephenson: Article written for *Medical Care*.

10. Undated reminiscences of Miss A. Scott, Elsie's Sister Tutor, West Suffolk General Hospital.

11. Civilian Relief File, Barnett Hill, British Red Cross Society (BRCS) Archives.

Chapter Three

1. *Instructions and Suggestions for Civilian Relief Workers*, BRCS Archives.

2. Dame Beryl Oliver, *The British Red Cross in Action,* Faber & Faber, London, 1966.

3. *Ibid.*

4. *Ibid.*

5. *Life Begins Again*, an account of activities of Civilian Relief Overseas Department, set up by the Joint War Organisation (JWO), and published by them.

6. Elsie Stephenson's report on Khatatba to Miss Fernandez and Dame Emily Blair, 5th August, 1944.

7. Elsie Stephenson, Sociology paper on "A Refugee Camp in Egypt", Toronto University, 1946-47.

8. *Ibid*.

9. *Ibid.*

10. *Ibid.*

11. *Ibid*.

12. *Ibid.*

13. Elsie Stephenson, Report on Khatatba, *Op. cit.*

14. Captain H. Ryan, Principal Medical Officer, Khatatba, Monthly Report for September, 1944.

15. JWO, *Life Begins Again, Op. cit.*

16. Elizabeth Nicolson to S. Allan.

17. Elsie Stephenson, Report on Khatatba, Op. cit.

18. Commissioned article for *Contact* magazine, entitled, "Grief in our Hospitals and our Homes,"

19. Louise Fraser, M.D. (St. Andrews) "Antenatal Work Among Yugoslav Refugees".

20. *Ibid.*

21. Captain H. Ryan, Monthly Report, *Op. cit.*

Chapter Four

1. Dame B. Oliver, *Op. cit.*, Chapter 3, Note 2.

2. Margot Lawrence, *Shadow of Swords*, Michael Joseph, 1971.

3. Dr. K. MacPhail to W. Gardner, 9.8.68.

4. American doctor's report to *Daily Mail* correspondent, quoted in *Shadow of Swords, Op. cit.*

5. *Newmarket Journal,* Thursday, 26th October, 1967.

6. David Mountfield, *The Partisans, Secret Armies of World War II*, Hamlyn, 1979.

7. M. Lawrence, *Op. cit.*

8. *The Picture History of World War II,* Grosset & Dunlap Publishers, New York, 1976.

9. Jean Bowden, *Grey Touched with Scarlet,* Robert Hale Ltd. London, 1959.

10. Mac Sopp to W. Gardner, ESC.

11. Peter Young, *World War 1939-1945*, Pan Books, London, 1966.

12. Report of Civilian Relief Discussion Group, Stockholm Red Cross Convention, 1948.

13. Elsie Stephenson to Dame Emily Blair, 2.2.45.

14. Mac Sopp to W. Gardner, *Op. cit.*

15. J. Bowden, *Op. cit.*

16. *Ibid.*

17. Elsie Stephenson, Report on Yugoslavia, March-June, 1945.

18. Newmarket Journal, *Op. cit.*

19. Dame B. Oliver, *Op. cit.*, Chapter 3, Note 2.

20. Elsie Stephenson, Report on Yugoslavia, *Op. cit.*

21. Jamieson, Sewall and Suhrie, *Trends in Nursing History,* Saunders, Philadelphia and London, 1966.

22. Elsie Stephenson's diary of World Health Organisation (WHO) tour, 1967.

Chapter Five

1. L. R. Seymer, *Op. cit.*, Chapter 2, Note 2.
2. J. Bowden, *Op. cit.*, Chapter 4, Note 9.
3. Rose van den Berg, Bad Munder, Joppe, Holland, November, 1967.
4. *Ibid*.
5. Wincenty Tylmonowski to S. Allan, 5.1.85.
6. Activity Report for period February 8th - February 26th, 1946, Bad Munder.
7. R. van den Berg, *Op. cit.*
8. W. Tylmonowski to S. Allen, 7.3.85.
9. Daisy Stroinski to W. Gardner, 25.4.68.
10. W. Tylmonowski to W. Gardner, 20.1.68.
ll German Red Cross Report on the plight of the refugees on the Eastern side of the Elbe, October 25th, 1945.
12. *Ibid.*
13. W. Tylmonowski to S. Allan, 5.1.85.
14. W. Tylmonowski to S. Allan, 7.3.85.
15. P. Young, *Op. cit.,* Chapter 4, Note 11.
16. Lord Woolton, "A World Work of Mercy", as reported in the *Sunday Times*, 5th September, 1948.

Chapter Six

1. Red Cross Report on North West Europe, Stockholm Conference, Notes, September, 1948.
2. Chairman, Civilian Relief Overseas to Elsie Stephenson, 1.3.46.
3. Report from Lisbeth Schmidt, arrived in Berlin from Silesia, 2.5.46, ESC.
4."Public Health" Report on the Nazi Health System, ESC.
5. W. R. Hughes, "Berlin and the Russians", ESC.
6. Report on Child Welfare Team's Work in Berlin, ESC.
7. Private visit report, Child Welfare Team, Berlin, 1946, ESC.
8. W.H.O. Seminar on Nursing Education for Child Care, Vienna, 1960.

Chapter Seven

1. H. E. Marshall, *Mary Adelaide Nutting: Pioneer of Modern Nursing,* Johns Hopkins University Press, Baltimore, 1972.
2. H. R. Hanley and M. Uprichard, *A Study of the Florence Nightingale International Foundation,* 1948.
3. W. Gardner's notes on interview with Eileen Rees, 19.6.68.

4. "A Year in Canada", E. Rees and E. Stephenson.

5. *First Elsie Stephenson Memorial Lecture,* The Canadian Scene, delivered by Professor Helen Carpenter, 14.3.73.

6. Charles Singer, Concept of Nursing, Toronto University.

7. *Ibid.*

8. Elsie Stephenson: Sociological Essay on French Canada, Public Health Advanced Course, 1.4.47.

9. *Canadian Nurse,* August, 1932.

10. J. F. Sleeman, *The Welfare State. Its Aims, Benefits and Costs,* George Allen & Unwin, London, 1973.

11. Notes on memories of Elsie by Eileen Rees, 19.6.68.

Chapter Eight

1. Elsie Stephenson, Personal Report on Germany - Hessen, November, 1947, to Miss Warner, Foreign Relations Department., B.R.C.S.

2. *Ibid.*

3. Paper on History of the German Red Cross, ESC.

4. Elsie Stephenson, Address on the History of Nursing, ESC.

5. *Ibid.*

6. Oberin Tobruth, Marburg, to Elsie Stephenson.

7. Diary of Miss Elsie Stephenson, Resident Organiser for North Borneo and Sarawak, B.R.C.S.

8. Elsie Stephenson, Report on Singapore, ESC.

9. Richard Hough (1983), *Edwina: Countess of Mountbatten of Burma,* Weidenfeld & Nicolson.

10. Diary.

11. Letter from Elsie Stephenson, Up River, Sarawak, 25.5.48.

12. The British Red Cross Travels East, Elsie Stephenson, Red Cross Quarterly Review, October, 1948.

13. W. Gardner to S. Allan, 8.12.75.

14. Dame B. Oliver, *Op. cit.,* Chapter 3, Note 2.

15. Elsie's lecture notes on Red Cross development and principles, ESC.

Chapter Nine

1. Dr. H. Rogers to W. Gardner, 2.1.69.

2. B. Abel Smith, *Op. cit.,* Chapter 1, Note 4.

3. General information on East Suffolk, ESC.

4. Elsie Stephenson to O. Baggally, 8.3.49.

5. M.V. Jones to W. Gardner, 10.11.68.

6. W. Gardner's notes on conversation with Dr. MacPhail, 9.8.68.

7. Alan Burgess, *The Lovely Sergeant,* Pan, London, 1963.

8. Margaret Brayton to S. Allan, 11.4.85.

9. Elsie Stephenson, *City and County of Newcastle,* National Health Service Annual Report.

10. "Director, Nursing Teaching Unit, University of Edinburgh", 20 April, 1956, in the *Nursing Times.*

11. "Concept of Nursing", Toronto University, ESC.

12. Memories of J. Geddes, Nurse Tutor, Newcastle General School of Nursing, 1955-57.

13. M. Freeman to S. Allan, *Op. Cit.,* Chapter 1, Note 5.

14. Miss A. Eden, Lecturer in education at Durham University, Jameson Report.

15. Elsie Stephenson, "The Application of Recent Research to Health Visiting", *Journal of the Royal Sanitary Institute,* Vol. LXXIII, No. 5, September, 1953.

16. Elsie Stephenson, *Report on Health Visiting,* Newcastle, 1955.

17. E. Wilkie to S. Allan, 15.2.85.

18. H.P. Pearey, Chairman, Newcastle-Upon-Tyne Women's Civic Committee to Elsie Stephenson, 1956.

19. Dame Catherine Scott to S. Allan, 17.10.85.

20. Dame Elizabeth Cockayne to S. Allan, 6.11.84.

21. H. Scharz to S. Allan, 12.6.84.

22. Dame E. Cockayne to S. Allan, *Op. cit.*

23. *An Inquiry Into Health Visiting,* Jameson Report, HMSO, London, 1956, Para. 306.

24. *Ibid,* Para. 348.

25. John Sheehan, from a series on Legislation, *Nursing Mirror,* 7.8.85.

26. Dame E. Cockayne, *Op. cit.*

Chapter Ten

1. Peta Allen and Moya Jolley, Eds. (1982) *Nursing, Midwifery and Health Visiting Since 1900,* Faber & Faber, London.

2. M. A. Nutting to Mary Roberts, 20.7.24, *Op. cit.,* Chapter 7, Note 1.

3. Gladys Carter (1939) *A Fair Deal for Nurses,* Gollancz, London.

4. P. Runciman, "The Shape of Things to Come", *Elsie Stephenson Memorial Lecture,* Nursing Mirror, September 9, 1981.

5. J. C. Geddes to S. Allan, 16.4.84.

6. Interview with M. Lamb by S. Allan, 14.11.84.

7. Minutes of the Senatus Academicus, University of Edinburgh, Vol. 14, Para. 120.

8. A. Kennedy to Elsie Stephenson, 25.3.56.

9. Professor Rosalind Mitchison, Associate Dean of the Faculty of Social Sciences, *Edinburgh University Bulletin*, June, 1983.

10. C. P. Snow, "The Two Cultures and the Scientific Revolution", delivered as the *Rede Lecture,* Cambridge, 1959, published that year and again in 1964.

11. E. Wilkie (1984) *Op. cit.,* Chapter 1, Note 20.

12. *Nursing Times,* Friday, 20th April, 1956.

13. Royal College of Nursing (RCN) to Elsie Stephenson, 10.5.56.

14. RCN Public Health Section to Elsie Stephenson, 25.4.56.

15. A. M. Currie, Secretary to the University, to S. Allan, 5.2.85.

16. *Minutes of the Senatus Academicus,* University of Edinburgh.

17. "Place of a nursing school in a university", Elsie's notes on her year in Toronto, ESC.

18. Kay Rowe to S. Allan, 28.3.85.

19. Margaret Lamb to S. Allan, 15.10.84.

20. M. Brayton to S. Allan, 15.10.84.

21. Elsie Stephenson to Ellen Broe, 28.2.57.

22. A. Altschul to S. Allan in interview, 17.9.84.

23. M. Thomson to S. Allan, in interview, 28.11.84.

24. N. Macdonald to S. Allan, 3.5.84.

25. Margaret Auld to S. Allan in interview, 15.2.84.

26. "An International School of Advanced Nursing Education at the University of Edinburgh," *Edinburgh University Gazette*, 1964.

27. Ibid.

28. Winifred Logan (1971 unpublished) "Integrated Degree/Nursing Programme, Survey of the Years 1960-70".

29. W. Logan to S. Allan in interview, 31.3.84.

30. F. Smith to S. Allan, 9.5.87.

31. Elisabeth Nicholson to S. Allan.

32. Sandra MacSwain, Janet Russell, Elisabeth Nicolson, Margaret Burnett to S. Allan.

33. Elsie Stephenson, Introduction to an article on research to be contributed by Dr. A.L. John, ESC.

34. Report: Nursing Studies Unit, ESC.

35. J. Macleod Clark and L. Hockey (1979) *Research for Nursing,* HM&M Publishers, Aylesbury.

36. Elsie Stephenson, "The Need for Nursing Research", *International Journal of Nursing Studies,* 2, 279, 1966.

37. Elsie Stephenson to Morley Joel, 21.2.64.

38. L. R. Seymer, *Op. cit.,* Chapter 2, Note 2.

Chapter Eleven
1. A. Altschul to S. Allan in interview, 17.9.84.
2. Jameson, Sewall and Suhrie, *Trends in Nursing History,* Saunders, Philadelphia and London, 1966.
3. Postcards in the ESC.
4. Acceptance form for W.H.O. Fellowship, ESC.
5. Elsie Stephenson to W. Gardner, 11.3.67.
6. Elsie Stephenson to W. Gardner, 14.3.67.
7. Vice Director of the Middle Medical Schools Department at the Ministry of Health and Social Welfare, Warsaw, to Elsie Stephenson, 21.1.67.
8. Elsie Stephenson to W. Gardner, 28.3.67.
9. Elsie Stephenson to W. Gardner, 2.4.67.
10. Elsie Stephenson to W. Gardner, 3.4.67.
11. Diary, 4.4.67.
12. Elsie Stephenson to W. Gardner, 7.4.67.
13. Diary, 9.4.67.
14. *Ibid.*
15. Diary, 14.4.67.
16. Diary, 17.4.67.

Chapter Twelve
1. E. Wilkie, *Op. Cit.,* Chapter 1, Note 20.
2. Elsie Stephenson to F. A. Wells, Secretary, Royal Society of Health, 30.6.64.
3. Elsie Stephenson to Miss Audrey Wood, General Secretary of the Royal College of Midwives, 7.8.64.
4. Robert Maxwell, Address to Public Health Nursing Section, Royal Society of Health Congress, Eastbourne, 30.4.65.
5. J. Elise Gordon, Memorial address in honour of Elsie Stephenson, Edinburgh, 1.11.67.
6. H. E. Marshall, *Op. cit.,* Chapter 7, Note 1.
7. Elsie Stephenson to Mr. Abrahart, Director of Extra-Mural Studies, Newcastle, 23.2.85.
8. Minutes of Scottish Sub-Committee of the Old Internationals' Association, 13.5.64.
9. W. Gardner to FNINA, Annual General Meeting, September, 1967.
10. *Glasgow Herald,* 15.1.85.
11. M. Tully, Pergamon Press to S. Allan, 4.4.85.

12. *International Journal of Nursing Studies,* Vol. 4, pp. 271-273, Pergamon Press, 1967.

13. A. D. Bell to Elsie Stephenson, 16.8.62.

14. Elsie Stephenson to Dr. Marcus, 15.6.62.

15. Elsie Stephenson to J. Brotherston, Usher Institute, Edinburgh, 23.6.62.

16. Editorial Bulletin, No. 2 in reference to meeting, 4.7.62.

17. A. Marcus to Elsie Stephenson, 13.11.62.

18. Elsie Stephenson to A. Marcus, 12.10.66.

Chapter Thirteen

1. Diary, 7.4.67.

2. Elsie Stephenson, Address to North Edinburgh Unionist Association, 24.7.64.

3. British Red Cross Society to Elsie Stephenson, 14.11.56.

4. Heidi Scharz to S. Allan, 11.6.84.

5. M. Freeman to S. Allan in interview, 17.4.84.

6. *Ibid.*

Chapter Fourteen

1. Quote From C. E. Winslow, used in Elsie Stephenson's address to the Health Visitors' Association Centenary, June, 1962.

2. Elsie Stephenson, Address to the Association of Hospital Matrons, Edinburgh Trained Tutors, March, 1963.

5. Elsie Stephenson, "Do you know your Colleagues?" ESC.

6. E. Wilkie to S. Allan, 15.2.85.

7. A. Altschul, Edinburgh, 6.4.84.

8. Report on W.H.O. Symposium on Education, Stuttgart, 1978.

9. Elsie Stephenson, lecture notes, ESC.

10. Elsie Stephenson to Health Visitor Centenary Conference, June, 1962.

11. Project 2000, United Kingdom Central Council, 1986.

12. M. Freeman to S. Allan, 18.4.84.

13. Elsie Stephenson to R. Maxwell, in preparation for his address to the Royal Society of Health, 1965.

BIBLIOGRAPHY

Abel-Smith, Brian, *A History of the Nursing Profession,* Heinemann Educational Books, Ltd., 1960 & 1966.

Allen, P., & Jolley, M. (Eds.) *Nursing, Midwifery and Health Visiting since 1900,* Faber & Faber, London, 1982.

Baly, Monica E., *Nursing and Social Change,* William Heinemann, Medical Books Ltd., London, 1973.

Bowden, Jean, *Grey Touched With Scarlet,* Robert Hale, London, 1959.

Burgess, Alan, *The Lovely Sergeant,* Heinemann, London, 1963.

Catford, E.F., *The Royal Infirmary of Edinburgh, 1929-1979,* Scottish Academic Press, Edinburgh, 1984.

Cook, Sir Edward, *The Life of Florence Nightingale,* Macmillan & Co. Ltd., London, 1914.

Davies, Christie, *Permissive Britain. Social Changes in the Sixties and Seventies,* Pitman, London, 1975.

Dow, Derek A., *The Rottenrow,* Parthenon Press, 1984.

Ferguson, Ron, *The Life of Geoffrey M. Shaw,* Famedram Publishers, Gartocharn, 1979.

Fisher, Richard B., *Joseph Lister 1827-1912,* Macdonald & Jane's, 1977.

Hasley, A.H., *Change in British Society,* Oxford University Press, 1978.

Hamilton, David, *The Healers. A History of Medicine in Scotland,* Canongate, Edinburgh, 1981.

Hough, Richard, *Edwina: Countess Mountbatten of Burma,* Weidenfeld & Nicolson, London, 1983.

Jameson Report, *An Inquiry into Health Visiting,* HMSO, London, 1956.

Jamieson, Sewall & Suhrie, *Trends in Nursing History,* Saunders, Philadelphia & London, 1966.

Kendall, Paul Murray, *The Art of Biography,* George Allen & Unwin, London, 1965.

Keneally, Thomas, *Schindler's Ark,* Coronet Books, Hodder & Stoughton, London, 1982.

King, Peter, *20th Century British History Made Simple,* W.H. Allen, London.

Lawrence, Margot, *Shadow of Swords.* A Biography of Elsie Inglis Michael Joseph, London, 1971.

Lewis, Peter, George Orwell - *The Road to 1984,* Heinemann Quixote Press, London, 1981.

Manton, Jo, *Elizabeth Garrett Anderson,* Methuen, London, 1965 & 1966.

Marshall, H.E., *Mary Adelaide Nutting: Pioneer of Modern Nursing,* Johns Hopkins Press, London & Baltimore, 1972.

Marwick, Arthur, *Britain in Our Century,* Thames & Hudson, London, 1984.

Mountfield, David, *The Partisans: Secret Armies of World War II,* Hamlyn, London, 1979.

McBryde, Brenda, Quiet Heroines. *Nurses of the Second World War*, Chatto & Windus, London, 1985.

Macdonald, Lyn, *The Roses of No Man's Land*, Michael Joseph, London, 1980.

McFarlane, Jean K., *The Proper Study of the Nurse*, R.C.N. Research Project, London, 1970.

Maclean, Fitzroy, *Tito: A Pictorial Biography*, Macmillan, London, 1980.

Oliver, Dame Beryl, *The British Red Cross in Action*, Faber & Faber, London, 1966.

Pavey, Agnes E., *The Story of the Growth of Nursing*, Faber & Faber, London, 1938-59.

The Picture History of World War II, Grosset & Dunlap, New York, 1976.

Seymer, Lucy Ridgeley, *A General History of Nursing*, Faber & Faber, London, 1961.

Runciman, Phyllis, Elsie Stephenson Memorial Lecture, published in *Nursing Mirror*, August 26 and September 9, 1981.

SHHD (Scottish Home & Health Department), *Continuing Education for the Nursing Profession in Scotland*, Edinburgh, 1981.

Shermer, *David, World War I*, Octopus Books, London, 1973.

Sleeman, J.F., *The Welfare State. Its Benefits, Aims and Costs*, George Allen & Unwin, London, 1973.

Smith, F. B., *Florence Nightingale. Reputation and Power*, Croom Helm, Kent, 1982.

University of Edinburgh, *Minutes of Senatus Academicus*.

Wilkie, Elaine, *A Singular Anomaly*. A Case Study of the Council for the Education and Training of Health Visitors, 1962 - 74, Royal College of Nursing, London, 1984.

Willcocks, A.J., *The Creation of the National Health Service*, Routledge & Kegan Paul, London, 1967.

Woodham-Smith, Cecil, *Florence Nightingale 1820 - 1910*, Constable, London, 1950 - 1961.

World Health Organisation, *Nursing Services*, Euro Reports & Studies 22, Stuttgart, 1978.

Young, Peter, *World War 1939-1945*, Arthur Barker, London, 1966.

ACKNOWLEDGEMENTS

I should like to thank most sincerely the following people who have helped me, with their recollections, their experience, and their encouragement.

Professor Annie Altschul, Miss R. E. Armstrong, Mrs. Audrey Atherton, Miss Margaret Auld, Mrs. Suzanne Baker, Dr. Monica Baly, Dr. Michael Barfoot, Mr. David Bayes, Sir John Brotherston (dec.), Miss Margaret Brayton, Dame Anne Bryans, Miss Mabel Burgess, Mrs. Margaret Burnett (nee Hewitt), Miss Cameron, Miss Norah Carr, Mrs. Jenny Causer (nee Lawson), Dame Elizabeth Cockayne, Adil Cook, Alex Currie, Dr. Celia Davies, Mlle. Genevieve Dechanoz, Miss Lesley deJean, Mrs. Joyce Double, Miss Margaret Freeman, Mr. Jimmy Geddes, Mrs.

Rosemary Gibson, Giffnock Library staff, Dr. Margaret Gilmore, Dr. David Hamilton, Miss Yvonne Hentsch, Miss Elizabeth Himsworth, Ms. Ann Holohan, Mrs. Constance Hold, King's Fund Centre, Miss Margaret Lamb, Mr. R. F. Matthew, Mr. Robert Maxwell, Mrs. Edna Mehen, Miss Brenda Moon, Miss Win Logan, Miss Nance Macdonald, Miss May McKean, Mrs. Sandra MacSwein (nee Lyall), Network Scotland, Mrs. Elisabeth Nicolson (nee Booth), Mrs. Margaret Poulter, Professor Penny Prophit, Mrs. Barbara Quaile, Mr. Hugh C. Rae, Miss Eileen Rees, Dr. Kay Rowe, Miss Phyllis Runciman, Mrs. Anne Russell (nee Wood), Mrs. Janet Russell (nee Robertson), Miss Heidi Scharz, Miss Agnes Scott, Dame Catherine Scott, Scottish Health Services Centre, Miss Helen Sinclair, Miss Margaret Slade, Professor Alan Steele, Mrs. Eileen Stephenson, Mr. Harry Stephenson, Mr. William Stephenson, Mr. Allan Story, Miss Margaret Thomson, Mr. Wincenty Tylmonowski, Mrs. Gillian Valentine, Miss Rose Van Den Berg, Miss Rosemary Weir, Miss Sarah Whitcher, Dr. Elaine Wilkie, Workers' Educational Association.

Edinburgh University's Department of Nursing Studies has offered support and encouragement, as well as providing financial help through the Gardner Bequest. The Carnegie Trust for the Universities of Scotland have given financial support toward publication of this biography. Without the notes collected by the late William Gardner, and now lodged in the Medical Archive Centre, High School Yards, Edinburgh, researching the biography would have been infinitely more difficult.

My family and friends have supported me with patience and encouragement. In particular, I should like to thank my father, Hugh C. Rae, and Rosemary Weir for reading and commenting on the manuscript.

I should also like to thank the publishers who have given me permission to quote copyright material: Gower, *A History of the Nursing Profession* by Brian Abel-Smith; Cambridge University Press, *The Two Cultures and the Scientific Revolution,* by C.P. Snow; Octopus Books, *World War I* by David Shermer; Weidenfeld & Nicolson, *World War 1939-1945* by Peter Young; Robert Hale, *Grey Touched with Scarlet,* by Jean Bowden; Johns Hopkins University Press, *Mary Adelaide Nutting: Pioneer of Modern Nursing,* by Helen E. Marshall; Faber & Faber, for *A General History of Nursing* by Lucy Seymer, *Nursing, Midwifery and Health Visiting Since 1900* by P. Allen & M. Jolley, *The British Red Cross in Action* by Dame Beryl Oliver, and *The Story of the Growth of Nursing* by Agnes Pavey; George Allen & Unwin, *The Welare State by* J.F. Sleeman; HMSO, The Jameson Report: *An Enquiry into Health Visiting;* Michael Joseph Ltd., *Shadow of Swords* by Margot Lawrence. Finally, I must admit defeat in being able to trace Gladys Carter who holds the rights for her book, *A Fair Deal for Nurses,* with the hope that she would not oppose references to it.